School Renewal

School Renewal

A Spiritual Journey for Change

Torin M. Finser, Ph.D.

ANTHROPOSOPHIC PRESS

Published by Anthroposophic Press
P.O. Box 799
Great Barrington, MA 01230
www.anthropress.org

Library of Congress Cataloging-in-Publication Data

Finser, Torin M., 1956– .
    School renewal : a spiritual journey for change / Torin M. Finser.
        p. cm.
    Includes bibliographical references.
    ISBN 0-88010-493-7
    1. Waldorf method of education. I. Title.

    LB1029.W34 F554 2001
    371.3—dc21

                                                        2001018921

10 9 8 7 6 5 4 3 2 1

Printed in the United States of America

Contents

Acknowledgments

I would like to thank the many teachers and parents in schools who took the time to share their thoughts, struggles, and hopes with me. I want to thank my students, present and former, at Antioch New England Graduate School and the Center for Anthroposophy. Special thanks go to Michael Dobson at the Anthroposophic Press for his encouragement and to those who support the Press with donations. I want to thank Lynda Smith-Cowan and Doreece Miller for their help with the original manuscript. Most of all, I want to wholeheartedly acknowledge the inspired work of my editor, Nicky Hearon, who helped me stretch, expand, rearrange, and clarify the text to help connect with the widest possible group of potential readers. Her additions, insights, and "life forces" are just as manifest in this book as are mine.

In addition, I thank my colleagues on the Teacher Education Committee of the Association of Waldorf Schools for the conversations that gave me material and enthusiasm for this project. Finally, I would like to thank my colleagues in the Collaborative Leadership Program for their insights, experience, and material included in several chapters of this book. May this effort support the growth and changes needed in our schools!

To my love
And all our children

1

INTRODUCTION

Stained-Glass Windows

Recently I found myself fulfilling a lifelong dream. My fiancée and I spent four days in Chartres, an immersion experience in the famous cathedral in France. During those wonderful days, we spent hours inside, walking the labyrinth, listening to music, visiting the crypt with the Black Madonna, and exploring virtually every nook and cranny. I was amazed at the tales told in stone and color, the history of the building, and the stories of those who taught there. We read books, asked questions, and visited the same locations again and again during those four days.

Sitting in a pew one afternoon, I found myself transfixed by the rose window, the wonder and wisdom before me. The light that came through the window was transforming; my breathing and feeling were affected. The space, both in the cathedral and within me, seemed full beyond expression. Overwhelmed, I went outside with the idea of walking around the cathedral. Almost by accident, I found myself stunned by a contrasting experience. From the outside, those same stained-glass windows were old, gray, and sooty. The stone façade was worn with weather and time. Standing back a few hundred yards, I took in the cathedral as a whole and understood it in a different way.

I was impressed with the contrast of the inner and outer experience of that afternoon. While sitting in the pew, I was filled with the richness of experience, caught up in the detail of the many stories. Outside, I gained perspective, saw the cathedral in the context of space and time, and experienced the human struggle in its creation.

School as a Journey was the story from the inside of a Waldorf school, the years I spent with my group as their class teacher. Working with the Waldorf curriculum day in and day out was not unlike being inside Chartres—the artistry, stories, and fullness of experience. Since graduating the class of 1990 in Great Barrington, I have worked differently. Teaching at Antioch graduate school has given me an opportunity to research, work with Waldorf and public school teachers, and visit interns in more than seventy-five schools. I have observed teachers growing and struggling and have been in schools that are healthy and others that are dysfunctional. My perspective has changed as I observe, compare, and consult.

We need both the inner and outer views to gain understanding. A creative tension can arise in which the struggle with questions can lead to new appreciation of what schools are all about. For me, the past few years have helped me place my classroom experiences in the context of larger school issues, such as governance, leadership, and community development. Living and learning are inseparable. Human beings participate in the continual flow of experiences. Through the ability to reflect, these experiences become knowledge. This process begins with the first breath of life and continues through the threshold of death.

Schools are merely a way of forming and organizing the learning experiences that society believes are necessary for children. As schools have grown and developed over the years, they have become more important as organizations, and sometimes the "living and learning" aspects have receded in favor of "expectations and requirements," whether imposed by legislators, parents, or textbook publishers. From time to time, when the structures in schools have become too rigid, courageous advocates for children have stepped forth to redress the balance.

Writers and educators such as Sylvia Ashton Warner, John Dewey, Ivan Illich, Herb Kohl, and others have tried to refocus our attention on the needs of the child. Waldorf education, founded in 1919 by Rudolf Steiner, is likewise a child-centered form of education.

The history of education tells the story of innovation that promotes life and of preservation that can promote structure. A new school or educational movement tends to be creative and exciting but chaotic, while schools that have been in existence for some time tend to be organized, predictable, and reliable in perpetuating traditions. Over the past years I often have wondered if there might not be a middle way, a third alternative between the bastion of conservatism represented in some older schools and the fresh-start approach of the new. Can one not find a way to have the benefits of both? After all, not everyone can start a school, and many feel the need to work with what is already there. Can schools be renewed?

The same dynamic often plays itself out in the biography of individual teachers. Although there are, of course, many exceptions, a new teacher typically will enter the classroom with considerable idealism and work with wonderful enthusiasm. This energy and striving can carry a new teacher through some of the hard knocks of classroom management and help the evolving teacher develop new inner resources as well as an age-appropriate curriculum. As time goes by, experience becomes a great ally, and the technique of teaching is fine-tuned to the point where a veteran teacher can hold a class with confidence and ease. Even the challenges (and children have a remarkable way of finding new ways to test us!) are in the context of previous experiences and are thus less overwhelming. Yet the veteran teacher also can become more conservative, opting for the tried and true, preserving the peace in the classroom, and doing what has worked in the past. Stability and order seem to become more important, and as we age, we try to conserve our resources. Like schools, teachers can experience the hardening influence of form and structure.

The discrepancy between the idealism of youth and the weight of maturity can become a trap for the teacher. The idealist and conservative live on in us, at times pulling in different directions. In trying to meet the many demands of school life, teachers can feel the fulfillment and satisfaction of earlier years waning. Many a teacher wonders: Can I continue? Do I have what it takes to meet the needs of these children? Where am I going in my own life? In countless interviews and conversations, I have heard the voices of teachers seeking renewal. This book is an attempt to share the stories of teachers and parents and my own experiences with schools.

Ewen's Heart Cup

When Ewen, my second son, was old enough to drink from a cup responsibly (not throw it on the floor or do any of the other delightful things a young child can do), we gave him a special cup that he adopted immediately. Blue on the inside and mostly white on the outside, this cup had colorful squares on portions of the exterior—green, violet, orange, yellow, and white. Best of all, about half of the squares were filled with hearts. Most were in complementary colors, and each heart was just big enough to fill a colorful square patch. Bold, bright, and friendly, this was a real child's cup. Ewen drank from this treasured cup for many years. It held his milk, herb tea, and, sometimes at night, hot chocolate. He always knew his place at the table by looking for his favorite cup, and woe befell the parent who forgot to set it out! He also took very special care of his cup; it was cleaned carefully, and, far from fading, the colors seemed to grow more exuberant as the years went by.

One day, another member of the family dropped this cup while washing dishes. The handle broke in several irreparable pieces, and, worst of all, there was a small hole in the side where the lower part of the handle had broken off. When he discovered the broken cup on the counter, Ewen was inconsolable. I held him in my arms to no avail. He kept on saying, "My heart cup. My heart cup." Finally, still choking on sobs, Ewen walked with me out to the barn to put his cup with the recyclables and trash. Grasping at any last strand of hope, I put it on the shelf instead of in the trashcan and said to Ewen, "Perhaps we will find something to do with this cup one day."

It sat on the barn shelf for two years, gathering cobwebs. The family went through divorce, and for a time I wondered where any of us would be. Then one day in early spring, I happened to pick up flower seeds and starter flats at a nursery, thinking that Ewen and I could start flowers indoors. We sat on the kitchen deck and filled the flats with soil. Then Ewen and I planted sunflower seeds, lupine, coreopsis, and other favorites. We had a few seeds left over, and on the spur of the moment, I went to the barn to see what else we could use for planting. When I returned with the old heart cup, there were smiles all around. Instead of strictly separating the seeds as we had done for the other flats, we just poured a bunch of seeds and soil into the heart cup, gave it water, and placed it on the windowsill over the kitchen sink.

I know there are common-sense explanations for things like this—more sunlight, water, and so on—but something remarkable happened. Although we had planted all the seeds at the same time with the same soil, the seeds in Ewen's heart cup came up first. Not only that, they grew into greener and more vibrant flowers than any of the others. Growing in a mixed bunch, they burst forth in chaotic exuberance. Full of life and joy, they were able to thrive in Ewen's heart cup until the time came for them to enter the perennial flowerbeds outside.

In many ways, this is the story I want to tell in *School Renewal*. This book is about dedication and hope, but it also tells of the hurt, the shadows, and the pain that can occur when teachers and parents strive to create a school community. As with many organizations, there are taboo subjects, ones that are felt and experienced but often not discussed. In this book I hope to make some of them discussible. In fact, some of the more difficult issues faced in school communities, if worked with, can become new substance for growth.

In contrast to my first book, *School as a Journey,* which described my journey as a classroom teacher and the unfolding curriculum of a Waldorf school, this book focuses on the issues and questions that arise outside the classroom. These issues include how we work together as adults, organizational issues, school leadership, community development, and the vital personal renewal that can make everything else possible. Our children look to parents and teachers as role models, not just in teaching reading and chemistry but also in the schooling of life. Can we become worthy of them?

Finally, I will say a few words about the structure of this book. Rather than giving recipes, I have chosen topics that can point in the direction of school renewal. Like a crystal with its many facets, the chapters focus on different aspects of school renewal. Each chapter is meant to be an invitation to explore further rather than a complete study. In fact, too much material actually can lead to "indigestion," which impedes flow, movement, process, and renewal. Rather than becoming learned "experts" on renewal, the important point is that we take up the suggestions and possibilities and put them into practice. For some readers, one pathway will be helpful, for others another. Because of the different biographies represented in a school community, renewal needs to be varied and multimodal. Instead of being arranged in the usual linear structure, the chapters are organized so that the reader can explore several topics and begin to see how they are mutually self-supporting, just as in a school all the entities—parent, teacher, and administration—are mutually interdependent. If we can recognize the key issues, learn new ways of working with them, and support each other in our common striving, we have a chance to create schools that are as vibrant as the children they serve!

2

SARAH'S STORY

One Day in the Life …

Sarah woke with a start. It was 6:45 a.m.! Had she turned off the alarm? Gone was the hour, her hour, the one hour she was counting on to get a head start on the day. The time to stretch, to find her center, and to prepare for the day. Now she would have to hurry.

Still dressing, she descended the stairs, calling to her children to wake up. Within moments, the kitchen was a flurry of activity; coffeemaker on, grapefruit and cereal laid out for breakfast, lunches still to be made—she would have to make them today, given the late start for the children. Between all the other activities, a quick call to the coach to see whether there would be a makeup game today for her son. As if he had a sixth sense that he was on her mind, her son, Colin, called down the stairs at this moment, "Mom, did you wash my jeans?" Not getting the reply he hoped for, he protested, "I have nothing else to wear! You know I hate my green cords! This sucks." Sarah's daughter, Rachel, came in with brush in hand for help with the knot in her hair. Somehow the family got out the door in time. Sarah even remembered to bring the map she had started for the geography section she was teaching.

During the half-hour drive to school, two conversations were going on, one with the children and one inside Sarah's head. "I must remember to call Sam's parents today. His homework hasn't been coming in. He seems tired and distracted. I need to know what is going on." At the same time, Rachel was asking, "Did you give me Jell-O today, Mom?" Sarah's thoughts turned to the lessons she would teach today. If only she had had more time to prepare. But she had been so tired last night. At least Mike would return from his sales trip tonight.

As Sarah entered the Waldorf School building, she remembered to go straight to her room. This technique always helped preserve the sanctity of the day. "No administrative distractions needed now. Let me just focus on my students." She had a few minutes to put up the half-finished map and straighten her desk before her fifth-graders began streaming in. Her spirits revived as she greeted them. Their fresh enthusiasm was contagious, and soon the room was a beehive of early morning chatter. Sarah felt confident and at home as she called the class to order and began her teaching day.

She was an experienced teacher and really enjoyed her work. The morning unfolded in a natural, seamless way, as she moved the group from one activity to another. On this particular morning, Sarah made two personal observations. First, as she opened the morning with the special verse they always used, she realized how much those lines nourished her as well as the class. She seemed to drink in each line, all the time wondering whether she was using this moment with the children to make up for the loss of her quiet time earlier. Second, she found herself once again marveling at the strengthening effect of rhythm. Her class knew the routine of the day. They counted on it. One could feel the sense of security it gave them. But Sarah realized this morning that she too was leaning on the routine for support. The word "leaning" gave her pause for thought. Was she leaning too much? Was she bringing enough new energy into the day? Was she resting on her experience and the rhythm of the day as a substitute for inadequate preparation? "I must not go down that road of self-doubt," she told herself, even as she wondered about how to renew her forces for the days ahead.

During recess, Sarah rushed to the office to call Sam's parents at work. The phone was busy. Along the way back down the hallway, she was stopped several times by colleagues who were upset with a change in the school calendar. Sarah wanted to join her class outside, so she did not pause to discuss anything. Yet the intensity of the hallway remarks rattled her. "I don't want to think about that stuff now," she said to herself, yet she was disturbed that she was thinking about it anyway. "We'll have to take it up in the meeting this afternoon." Her class was glad to see her appear outside, and immediately some of the girls pulled her into their game of dodgeball for all of the five minutes left in recess.

Math class went well, but instead of her free period before lunch, Sarah had to substitute for the French teacher, who was sick again. "How is it that some people can afford to be sick?" thought Sarah as she got her students going on a project. She helped Sam with his homework while eating lunch with her class. She did manage to finish her apple.

After school dismissal that day, when Rachel and Colin were safely off to their after-school activities, Sarah had five minutes to discuss the calendar issue with the chair of the afternoon meeting. Waldorf schools practice self-administration, which means that the teachers carry a large portion of the day-to-day tasks, such as scheduling, hiring, outreach, and admissions. Most Waldorf schools have faculty meetings once a week, supplemented by committee meetings and the long-range work of the College of Teachers. The faculty's spending time together after hours is vital to the success of the school. The committee meetings went smoothly—Sarah was good at this sort of thing—and then the whole faculty gathered from four to six in the afternoon for professional development work. On this particular afternoon, the faculty engaged in one of Sarah's favorite artistic activities, a form of movement called eurythmy. Simply moving in and out of the circle, using her arms to shape the sounds, gave Sarah new strength. "This is what I needed. I am so glad I teach here," she thought.

The business portion of the meeting was contentious, however. The calendar was the hot topic, which could be sensed even as reports were given on other matters. When the topic finally came up for discussion, there was little time left for a full airing of concerns, and under time constraints people repeated themselves. Sarah observed that the facilitator gave up part way through the session and that many colleagues were stating positions rather than problem solving. As everyone grew more tired, personalities stepped forward, and the sense of serving the school diminished. "No wonder," thought Sarah. "Few of us really have any training in self-administration and group work, so we have to go through all these frustrating experiences." She offered a few suggestions that were not really acknowledged, so she remained quiet for the rest of the meeting. In the end the issue was sent out to committee.

It was a weary Sarah who drove home with her two children at six that evening. She had an idea or two about supper—Colin could be counted on to help. Anything to do with food was of interest to him. And Mike would be home later. Even when he was tired, he usually did the dishes and helped with homework and bedtime preparations. It was nine p.m. before Sarah sat down at her desk to prepare the next day's lesson. The compositions would have to be corrected another day, "perhaps tomorrow in my free period, *if* the French teacher is back." Sarah went straight to the heart of her geography lesson, but by ten o'clock she started nodding off while reading. "I'll get up early tomorrow morning, but I must remember not to turn off the alarm."

Three Years Later ...

It was during an open house that Joan first noticed the change. In hindsight, she should have known sooner, but life was so hectic; it was hard to take in everything. But here she was, at this public event, watching Sarah do what Sarah had always done so well—welcome parents and introduce the afternoon's events. Joan had made sure her class was settled into their seats, stopped a few whispers, and was now free to attend to what Sarah was saying. Suddenly it struck her. Something was wrong. Sarah seemed different, at first in imperceptible ways. Yet Joan knew her well, they had taught together in the same school for years, and their families often spent vacations together. What was different this morning?

Sarah seemed distant, distracted. Her speech was disjointed and slurred at times. With one hand she kept brushing back her hair, and with the other she fumbled with her program. She had to clear her throat several times and moisten her lips as if she had been speaking for hours. What was wrong? Joan made a mental note to seek her out later. Ken first noticed a change during the snack break of the faculty meeting when he asked Sarah about a seemingly minor detail, and she burst out: "I CAN'T BE EVERYTHING TO EVERYBODY!" Shocked, Ken backed off, but felt hurt and mystified.

At home her husband noticed that Sarah's language had changed subtly. Previously upbeat and optimistic, she now relied on negative forms of communication: "I'll never finish this project. I don't think the school is in a good place. I hate feeling rushed all the time." Sarah's children complained, "Mom, you never do anything with us anymore." These were just the outer symptoms, however. Inside, Sarah was going through far more than her friends, colleagues, and family realized. Writing in her journal that week, Sarah poured out her heart:

"Something is wrong, but I don't exactly know what it is. After so many years of teaching, I should be able to shine, but it seems that each day I fall further behind. I know how things should be, but I continually fall short. Are my expectations too high? Am I really meant to be a teacher? I hate the constant feeling of not quite achieving what I had planned, hoped for, imagined. Occasionally I see myself as if in a mirror and am shocked. I am never able to do enough, and something inside mocks me for that.

"This year the parents really irritate me with their insidious questions and doubts. I love the children, always have, but my tolerance for their persistent quirks and particular mannerisms seems to be waning. The school is actually dysfunctional. What do they think they are doing with all those meetings? Don't they see how pointless it is? Most people do what they want anyway, regardless of what was decided. Whatever I say doesn't seem to make a difference. Is this the right place for me?

"I feel emotionally exhausted. It used to be that a good night's sleep or a long walk would put things right again. It is frightening, really, but these things no longer seem to work. I am losing my relationship with my colleagues, am irritated by the parents, and my children feel abandoned. Mike has stopped asking me to go out on the weekend. What has happened to my life?"

Not long after this journal entry, Sarah came down with pneumonia. She spent many weeks immobile, miserable, and ever so sick. At times all she could do was stare at the paintings on the wall of her room. After a partial recovery, she had a relapse. She was out of school for several months. It was clearly a time for reassessment. How would she emerge? Could she resume teaching? Would there be a change in her life, her way of living?

Meanwhile, Back at School ...

While Sarah was home with pneumonia, the school was going through its own crisis. Through all sorts of wind and weather the parents of the Morning Glory Waldorf School had been there. They had found the land, helped with the clearing, raised sums of money none had dreamed possible, and built the school, in many cases with their own hands. They had served as class reps, were available to chaperone field trips even when that meant taking off a day from work, and served on committees and the board of trustees. As the teachers often acknowledged, the school would not be there had it not been for the parents.

But lately something seemed to be changing. Partly it was demographic. The children of the first generation of parents had graduated from the eighth grade. Those who were left were tired, and their own lives had changed: job promotions made life more hectic, and some had been through divorce or separation. In some cases, the lead parents were just not willing to "put out" for the school anymore.

But there were other currents at work. Many parents had come to resent the attitude of certain teachers, who seemed to say, "We accept you on our terms only." Some parents experienced this as a condescending manner, as if the teacher were the highest on the food chain and knew best on every subject. Further, the parents found that communication was sorely lacking—events and policy changes were shared late and often in an inarticulate manner. It seemed that the faculty made decisions to please the teachers and often failed to think of the parents. Calendar dates and times were changed at will, causing tremendous hardship to working mothers and fathers. At the board level, the faculty seemed grateful for donations and volunteer time, but when there was a real issue, such as a budget line item for scholarships, the parent members of the board felt that their views were discounted. There were numerous former board members in the community who spoke openly about the power and control issues at the school.

As often happens, one event served as a catalyst for parent discontent. For more than a year, the third grade had been struggling. Children went home complaining, parents seemed to find the teacher unapproachable, and the faculty spent considerable time trying to cope. Classroom management was at the heart of the issue, and two children were seen as the ringleaders. These boys, who gave all their teachers a hard time, responded only if given lots of personal attention and seemed intent on disrupting every lesson. Of late their behavior and the teacher's inability to work with them was evident even during the assemblies. Parents noticed and expressed their concern, both to the teachers and to each other, which seemed only to increase the problem. After lengthy meetings, the faculty decided to ask one boy to leave the school, effective the following Monday. The parents of the child were informed in a late-night phone call from a teacher who clearly had been through a lot and did not have the time or energy to speak with them at length. The parents of this boy were devastated—they had given many years to the school only to be "dismissed" in a single day. Didn't the school bear some responsibility for letting the problem go on so long? Where was faculty accountability?

The sadness of the mother and father was nothing, however, compared with the outrage at the perceived injustice that swept through the rest of the parent body. The parents felt that they had not been given all the facts, and nobody seemed interested in explaining them. Did the teachers believe that after years of working with parents to foster community and build a sense of belonging the parents, in this instance, could just abandon their feelings and shared commitment? The situation became even more poisoned when the parents realized that of the two challenging boys, the one not asked to leave was a faculty member's child. Some of the parents asked for a meeting with the teachers. Upon being challenged, the faculty closed ranks and did not respond other than to place a self-righteous statement in the weekly bulletin affirming the pedagogical prerogatives of the teachers in a faculty-run school. Parents felt used and abused.

The school's deficit was growing, in part because of an increase in scholarships, late payments of student tuition, and the failure of the annual appeal to generate donations. After years of use, the building was now in need of attention, and positions had been created faster than salaries had increased. Unlike previous years when there had been deficits, board members now seemed disconnected from the problem. Whenever the deficit came up as an issue, it was sent back to another committee for more information. Everyone seemed to be avoiding the problem or at least appeared to be unwilling to confront it.

Finally, this Waldorf School had absorbed an unusual number of newly trained teachers in the past two years, individuals who were in need of mentoring. Yet the informal, casual system of mentoring that had been in place since the early days no longer seemed adequate. The faculty, already stretched thin, needed a new impulse in mentoring and evaluation.

But under all these "presenting" issues, a more fundamental concern lurked among the teachers: developing the mentoring program, balancing the budget, and forging a healthy partnership between parents and teachers required energy and time that simply were not available. In part, people just seemed perpetually busy and inwardly distracted. Beyond that, their central purpose and vision seemed to be waning. Levels of frustration had built up. Some teachers really were focused just on their classes, and others were unwilling to step forward out of fear of being cut down. Furthermore, there were questions hovering, often unspoken but nevertheless felt whenever there was a meeting: What do we mean by "faculty-run school" or "self-administration"? How can we develop the skills to carry out our vision of the school, build trust and confidence, and develop community? What kind of leadership do we need at this stage of the school's life? To those who were conscious of these questions, it was clear that a quick fix of the surface challenges (such as the deficit and student expulsion) would not work unless the fundamental issues of school governance and leadership were addressed.

As a key member of the school community, Sarah had been experiencing, even absorbing, some of these challenges long before they became conscious. Her personal talents were used to the maximum, and she and others surprised themselves with what they could do in "keeping things afloat" with minimal time and expertise. What was lacking in training and preparation was made up in the expenditure of human resources. This was one reason the school had functioned so well for so many years.

And yet Sarah was also part of the problem. By extending herself again and again, she took on, in a personal way, things that could have been owned by the group. By taking on more than was healthy for one person, her immune system was gradually weakened. Waldorf educators speak of *life forces* that replenish and renew the human being. When life forces are weakened, as with too little sleep, overwork, and stress, the immune system is affected, and one is more susceptible to illness. The process can be gradual, yet there is often a general weakening: one is less able to multitask, anxiety increases, and the emotional life becomes more volatile. Above all, one is simply less successful in doing what one has previously done so well. As Sarah became less able to keep up with her work, the administrative tasks she carried were not attended to, and various parts of the school did not function as before. A gap emerged between what people thought was happening, based upon past experiences, and what was actually occurring. No single person knew what was wrong, and the meetings did not yield the data that would have given a full picture of the state of the Morning Glory Waldorf School. As Sarah's immune system weakened, the organizational life of the school deteriorated. Her health and that of the school were intertwined.

It was not surprising that the body finally gave way. Stress that becomes distress eventually affects the immune system. The story of Sarah is not rare; most teachers experience one or more of the symptoms portrayed here, though they often are unrecognized. The problem may be sensed in a vague, general way, but the severity of particular instances can go unnoticed for a long time. Meanwhile the affected teacher influences the quality of decision making at the school, relations with parents and the community, and, most important, the contact with the children. It is hard to teach well if you yourself are not well. The health of teachers and the health of a school matter more than one might realize. Children absorb everything. They know, they respond, and they are affected.

As with most things in life, the most important initial step is recognizing the phenomenon, seeing what is really there, and knowing the symptoms when they arise. Sarah showed many of the classic signs of stress:

- Feelings of helplessness, frustration, even anger;

- Negative thoughts, language, feelings; general disillusionment;

- A growing gap between expectations and perceived reality;

- Low sense of personal accomplishment, which can hamper motivation and lead to greater fatigue, creating experiences of failure that might be referred to as "learned helplessness";

- Diminished social life, detachment, distancing from friends, family, colleagues;

- Less idealism, growing self-absorption and cynicism;

- Absenteeism or at least situations where the teacher may be present physically but is inwardly somewhere else.

It is important to note that stress is an everyday phenomenon; everyone experiences stress of one sort or another. It is the buildup and accumulation of events that can bring lasting damage, even burnout. Most people recognize the major life stresses and rally around a friend when there is a death in the family, a divorce, or a housing change. Yet the steady accumulation of minor stresses can be just as dangerous, especially because they often go unobserved. As we saw, when the life forces, that essential quality of growth, are depleted over time, the immune system eventually is weakened, and physical illness can develop.

Teachers often report schoolwide or institutional sources of stress, such as classroom discipline, administrative pressures, difficult parents, role conflict and ambiguity, professional isolation, lack of career advancement and professional growth, high demands coupled with low resources to meet them, interpersonal problems, and unresolved conflict. Public school teachers, in particular, report resistance to regulations and procedures, low participation in decision making, lack of freedom, and the absence of social or community support networks for teachers.

The demographics of teacher burnout give us a picture of the types of teachers at greatest risk. They include those who are young, teachers at the junior-high and high-school levels, men, single teachers, teachers in rural schools, and those with negative attitudes. That so many teachers are represented in the demographics of burnout indicates a gap between the expectations of the parents and administration and the perceived reality of the teacher. This gap grows so wide that at some point the abyss opens up and the bewildered teacher falls through.

I often have experienced the gap between expectation and reality. To some extent this is part of life and can lead to humility and the effort to better oneself. But at other times the gap is too great, and the feeling of inadequacy can become corrosive. Some years ago I had to give a talk at a university. My usual format is part presentation, part workshop, in which the participants join in the process through activities, questions, and conversation. But in this case I was told that the talk would be in a large lecture hall with fixed seats; the students were enrolled in education programs and had no previous background in Waldorf education. My anxiety only increased when I visited the building ahead of time and found the room to be cold, with cinderblock walls and tiers of seats. It seemed that what was expected of me, coupled with the format and the structure of the room, was leading me to be something I did not want to be—a lecturer. There was a great difference between what I was able to give and what I was asked to give. The experience of this gap gave me a hollow feeling, and for a while I was paralyzed and unable to prepare.

In the end I found a way to make the presentation with singing and concentration exercises involving rhythmic clapping. I learned an important lesson from experiencing this gap between expectation and reality. What I feel within myself—my sense of confidence and ability to meet the expectation of my work—is vitally important to what I am able to accomplish. And whether I am confident in my work or lost in confusion affects the health of the school or institution with which I work.

Thus my inner well-being is a spiritual issue. We have all seen or been part of a tired, disillusioned group. Then, suddenly, with the addition of one new member with vibrant energy and enthusiasm, the group begins to change! People often attribute this positive change in a group to the personality of the new member. I think that is overly simplistic. It is also the spiritual path and life intentions of the new person that speak to the group in every glance, phrase, and gesture. It matters ever so much who joins us in a school. In every hiring decision, rather than just filling a job, we also are filling a human position. And that human position speaks to parents and teachers alike, either enhancing or detracting from the health of the community. We need to look for human beings who can help us with social tasks in a particular school, and when we are fortunate enough to find the person with the needed capacities, the rest of us are given the stimulus to develop ours further.

Nowhere to Go

In those weeks at home, during one of her lucid moments, Sarah found herself saying, "It is gone—my class, my work. I am all alone." What had been a life full of relationships to people with all sorts of shared experiences was reduced to a room with four walls, a bed, and many hours of contemplation. Sarah realized that her former life had ended. The security of routine, the crowded days with unsorted experiences, the many details—it was all gone. Instead there was now an empty space. Sarah felt small in that space.

Then the question arose, "So, then, who am I?" Her self had been defined for so long by her roles—mother, teacher, wife, organizer. Her outer circumstances had formed her, shaped her inner life, even her thoughts. Her world had been full of what everybody else wanted her to be. And she had been there to please and support others. Now, at this time of illness, she had to confront the question: "Who am I, and what am I supposed to be doing with my life?"

Again and again she asked herself this question; it reverberated through her like a bell. She felt that she needed an answer before she could rebuild. Some days later, while she was sitting in her rocker leafing through the family Bible, Sarah found a few words from the Gospel of Matthew that came off the page and went right into her heart: "And, lo, I am with you always, even unto the end of the world" (Matt. 28:20). These words were infinitely comforting. This led her, in turn, to thoughts of the Native American elder who had come to her classroom and told stories to the children. The elder had explained to the children that native people never feel alone. They believe there is energy and spirit in all things. This is why native people refer to living things as "all my relations," whether it is a tree, a bird, or a stone. The elder also had said that everything, including human beings, is part of what native people refer to as the Greater Mystery, and therefore we need never feel isolated or without help. When our burdens seem too heavy, it is time to look for something greater than we are ourselves. These thoughts and words held a clue, a little seed that Sarah knew she could nurture and grow in time. She realized that she could not solve her concerns and problems by herself; they were a clue to her own journey of spirit. She put her head back and slept as she had not slept for a long time.

In the coming weeks and months, Sarah took up the task of personal renewal with the same commitment and determination she had given to everything else in her life. She decided not to return to teaching until she could become a new person—and not just in terms of her physical health. She soon realized that she was not alone in her challenges. Numerous colleagues shared aspects of the imbalance that had finally brought her down. Her quest, for that is what it soon became, was more than personal. She realized that by taking care of herself, she would truly be doing a service to her colleagues and the whole school. Her first step was to learn what had happened to her. She needed to explore the shadows as well as the opportunities for growth.

The chapters that follow contain the results of Sarah's search for renewal, a process that took her to many unexpected places. Exploring the unknown was, in fact, an essential part of her spiritual journey. If we routinely work with what is already known, we skim the surface of deeper realities. Teachers in particular have to guard against this tendency, for in the press of preparation and the need to articulate and share immediately what has just been assimilated, there is a natural bias toward the conscious pole of life. In this focus, however, inner resources can be used up. Rather than continually concentrating on what one already knows, it is best to take real risks occasionally with regard to one's soul. This is what Sarah courageously decided to do.

The topics covered in the rest of this book can be viewed as the advice Sarah and other teachers and parents have shared with me over several years of working with schools. There is no recipe or road map to school renewal, but the shared experiences indicate that there are certain pathways that can lead to rebirth. These pathways are not linear but elliptical in nature. We meet experiences that can give us the courage to continue spiritual explorations.

3

IT'S A BALANCING ACT

....

Two Companions on the Journey

    On the shores of the Mediterranean the sun really knows how to shine. It is so powerful that it tans the people a mahogany brown; and the young scholar who came from the north, where all the people are as white as bakers' apprentices, soon learned to regard his old friend the shadow with suspicion. In the south one stays inside during most of the day with the doors and shutters closed. The houses looked as if everyone was asleep or no one was at home. The young foreigner felt as if he were in prison, and his shadow rolled itself up until it was smaller than it had ever been before. But as soon as the sun set and a candle lighted the room, out came the shadow again. It was truly a pleasure to watch it grow; up the wall it would stretch itself until its head almost reached the ceiling ....

    The next evening the scholar was sitting as usual on his balcony. From his room the lamp burned brightly, and since his shadow was very shy of light, it had stretched itself until it reached the opposite balcony. When the young man moved, his shadow moved. "I believe my shadow is the only living thing over there," he muttered. "See how it has sat down among the flowers. The balcony door is ajar. Now if my shadow were clever, it would go inside and take a look around; then it would come back and tell me what it had seen. Yes, you ought to earn your keep." he said

*jokingly. "Now go inside. Did you hear me? Go!" And he nodded
to his shadow and his shadow nodded back at him. "Yes, go! But
remember to come back again." There the scholar's conversation
with his shadow ended. The young man rose, and the shadow on
the opposite balcony rose; the young man turned around and the
shadow also turned around; but then something happened there
that no one saw. The shadow went into his own room and closed
the drapes behind him.*

*The next morning on his way to the café where he had his
breakfast and read the newspapers, the scholar discovered that he
had no shadow. "So it really went away last night!" he marveled.*

*Settled once more in his own country, the scholar wrote books
about all that is true and beautiful and good. The days became
years. The scholar was now a philosopher; and the years became
many. One evening when he was sitting alone in his room there was
a very gentle knock at the door.*

*"Come in," he called. But no one came, so the philosopher
opened the door himself. Before him stood the thinnest man that he
had ever seen, and, judging from his clothes, a person of some
importance. "Whom do I have the honor of addressing?" the philosopher asked.*

*"I thought as much," replied the stranger. "You don't recognize
me, now that I have a body of my own and clothes to boot. You
never would have believed that you would meet your old shadow
again. Things have gone well for me since we parted. If need be, I
can buy my freedom!" The shadow jiggled its purse, which was filled
with gold pieces, and touched the heavy gold chain that it wore
around its neck. On all of its fingers were diamond rings, and every
one was genuine.*

*"I must be dreaming!" exclaimed the philosopher. "What is
happening?"*

*"Well, it isn't something that happens every day," said the
shadow, "but then you're not an ordinary person. Nobody knows
that better than I do, didn't I walk in your first footsteps? As soon
as you found that I could stand alone in the world, you let me go.*

The results are obvious. Without bragging, I can say few could have done better....

"I came out only in the evening; then I would walk around in the moonlight, stretching myself up the walls to get the kinks out of my back. Up and down the streets I went, peeping through the windows of the attics as well as the drawing rooms. And I saw what no one ever sees, what no one ever should see! It's really a horrible world, and I wouldn't be human if it weren't so desirable. I saw things that ought to be unthinkable; and these were not only done by husbands and wives, but by parents and the sweet, innocent children I saw." Said the shadow, "I saw everything that man must not know, but what he most ardently wishes to know— his neighbor's evil! If I had written a newspaper, everyone would have read it; but instead I wrote directly to the persons themselves, and I wreaked havoc in every city that I came to. People feared me so much and were so fond of me! The universities gave me honorary degrees, the tailors gave me clothes, and the women said that I was handsome. In a word each donated what he could, and so I became the man that I am.... But it is getting late, and I must say goodbye. Here is my card. I live on the sunnier side of the street and am always home when it rains."...*

Matters did not improve for the philosopher; on the contrary, sorrow and misery had attached themselves to his coattails. For the most part, whenever he spoke of the true and the beautiful and the good, it was like setting roses before a cow. Finally he became seriously ill. "You look like a shadow of your former self," people would say, and when he heard these words a shiver went down his spine.*

"You ought to go to a health resort," suggested the shadow when it came to visit him again. "There's no other alternative. I will take you along for old time's sake. I'll pay the expenses, and you'll talk and try to amuse me along the journey. I'm going to a spa myself, because my beard won't grow. That's a disease too, you know, because beards are a necessity. If you're sensible, you'll accept. We'll travel as friends."*

And so they traveled; the shadow as master and the master as shadow. For whether they were being driven in a coach, riding horseback, or simply walking, they were always side by side and the shadow kept itself a little in the fore or in the rear, according to the direction of the sun. It knew how to create the impression that it was the superior...."

"How strange!" remarked the philosopher after the shadow had left.[1]

It is remarkable how we often set ourselves up for our worst fear so that eventually we are forced to confront it. It is almost as if there is an intention behind our incompleteness, a tendency to become so caught in particular habits that we have to break out and reverse course.

As Sarah soon realized in her search for renewal, her complacency had been her worst enemy. It took her illness to shake her up, to reexamine not only what she was doing but also how she was living. Her collapse was the result of an accumulation over years. She needed to put aside the education she practiced in school each day and take up self-education. Some people might approach things in a superficial way and imagine that it is simply a matter of overcoming the illness or perhaps evading or avoiding it. This does not work, especially with entrenched habits. Sarah could not transform her old habits of enabling, making do with little, and rushing through experiences rather than living them until she really had possessed them and embraced them fully.

Reading fairy tales, Sarah came across one she had not noticed before. Portions of the story, by Hans Christian Andersen, are quoted at the beginning of this chapter. So it was at an early stage in her recovery that Sarah met a particular companion who had been following her in her life journey—her shadow. As she reviewed her interactions with colleagues and the many meetings she had experienced through the years, she could now recognize some of the shadow interactions that so often had brought her particular frustration, in large part because she did not completely see what was happening at the time. Living in half-knowledge is often the most frustrating experience. It leaves one with a vague sense of unease, but because there is less than full clarity, it lingers in one's consciousness, lurking there even as one is performing other tasks or trying to go to sleep at night. Sarah recognized that despite the warm, collegial relations she had experienced for the most part, there also had been "negative" energies that had played into those interactions: moments of real hostility, occasional power conflicts, and even inappropriate personal relationships. These shadow experiences had been sensed but not worked with. There was almost an unwritten rule not to acknowledge them. As a consequence, they at times became larger than life. In his book *The Archetypes and the Collective Unconscious*, C. G. Jung has this remarkable description:

> The shadow personifies everything that the subject refuses to acknowledge about himself and yet is always thrusting itself upon him directly or indirectly—for instance, inferior traits of character and other incompatible tendencies. This inferior part of the personality with both good and reprehensible tendencies is incompatible with the chosen conscious attitude. Thus it is often denied expression in life and therefore tends to coalesce into a relatively autonomous splinter personality with contrary tendencies in the unconscious. The shadow behaves compensatorily to consciousness.[2]

A kind of self-deception can occur when the shadowy double is able to exist alongside the higher self or *I* but is not recognized. It is as if one sees the "light" aspects without integrating the "dark" aspects of the personality. The result of self-deception is that the shadow leads the soul into a second, unhealthy life that surprises and confounds our human striving. Especially in the teaching profession, where individuals are working out of love of the children and spiritual idealism, it is possible to have the shadow play a stronger role than one might imagine. As was the case with Sarah, many teachers work to create a healthy, holistic environment for the children, yet often give less attention to the integration of the shadow aspect of the self. The easiest, most natural tendency is to ignore aspects of oneself and devote full energy to nourishing others. After all, there is much that one finds in the shadow that can be shameful, ugly, or even frightening. But the shadow also can contain positive qualities, such as normal instincts, appropriate reactions, realistic insights, and even creative impulses. One needs both the light and the dark to experience color and diversity.

As a result of these readings and reflections, Sarah resolved to reexamine herself in light of the descriptions of human nature that Rudolf Steiner referred to as the astral or emotional body. Steiner suggested that we share this trait in common with animals—a sensitivity to our environment and our emotional and feeling life. This sensitivity to our environment allows us to be conscious of our thoughts, feelings, and impulses. Sarah decided that she needed to understand better the feeling life in general, including the sympathies and antipathies that work in human interactions. But before doing so, she identified a few questions to help her more consciously recognize her own shadow and that of others in the future:

- Is there a lack of clarity in my relationship with a particular person?

- Am I sensing a lack of clarity between two people in my environment that can affect the work of the school?

- If I experience strong feelings, where are they coming from?

- How much of this feeling perception is coming from me, and how much truly is stimulated from without?

• What can I do to clear my emotions and do my personal work before reentering a particular meeting?

• Am I constantly working out of the same "gesture," the same habit or old way of doing things? Am I able to call upon a more complete spiritual experience that allows for the practice of health?

• If the unspoken consensus often is not to look at "shadows" (either individual or school shadows), how can I find the right question to bring the issue into the light of consciousness?

• Can I use my consciousness and my inner struggle to build new scaffolding of light and meaning for daily living?

• How can I help create a climate in our school in which people can truly communicate on all levels?

• How can I help those around me realize that integration of all aspects of oneself is necessary for healthy teaching and living?

Another Companion

It was a particularly bright day in early spring when Sarah was able to sit outside on her porch for the first time in many weeks. Wrapped in her afghan, she gently rocked back and forth and marveled at the budding trees, bright daffodils, and greening grass. Her senses seemed newly awakened; the colors, sounds, even the taste of that spring day seemed richer than before. Sarah sensed these impressions with a new awareness. Marveling at this beauty, she remembered lines from a lecture she had read years ago, in which Steiner stated: "Our Angel dwells in the Sun's rays which penetrate our eyes, making objects visible.... The Beings of the Angels live in waves of sound, the rays of light and color and in other sense perceptions."[3]

Why did this thought come back to her just now? What was the meaning of this statement? Who is this Angel that dwells even in nature? She then thought of the African folktale of Elegba, the trickster who wears a hat that is black on one side and green on the other. Walking down the road one day, Elegba causes two men on opposite sides of the road to get into an argument. One is convinced that he has seen Elegba in a green hat. The other is convinced that he has seen Elegba in a black hat. Elegba just laughs because his hat is both green and black. This duality of black and white, good and evil is found in every culture. Sally decided to explore these questions more deeply in the days of convalescence ahead.

She found references in the *Meditations* of Marcus Aurelius, a Roman emperor and Stoic philosopher of the second century A.D., to the "demon" seen as a Leader Being. Zeus himself gave this Leader Being to humans as a particle of his very own nature. Taking up other sources, she found that the Romans frequently referred to the "genius" to whom men of prominence, in particular, were indebted for inspirations and special abilities. The Greeks and then the early Christians used the term "angels" to describe the "proclaimer" or messenger of God. Peoples in northern Europe spoke of the Valkyries, the virgins with their gleaming coats of mail and swan wings that guided the destiny of battle. The Greek philosopher Socrates described his living exchanges with a higher Thou, which gave him advice and much wisdom right through his time of imprisonment. Socrates felt that he could entrust himself to this higher being that stood as a mediator between the earthly and the divine spheres.[4]

Sarah also read Alice O. Howell's book *The Dove and the Stone* on finding the sacred in the commonplace. She especially liked the definition of this angelic quality or divine essence as the "divine guest" that resides in each and every human being. As a Waldorf teacher, Sarah was drawn particularly to the writings of Rudolf Steiner. The following passage in *Man and His Angel*, by Richard Meyer, which quotes Steiner, truly spoke to the heart of the striving teacher:

One can develop the exercise of looking upon the lives of one's fellow men, and the expressions of their character, with the eyes of their angels, with that trusting glance directed to what is in process of becoming." Steiner once described in a conversation the hidden effects that the angel has in the soul of man: "The angels want to release ideals for the future within them," and through the pictures that they let sink into the souls of sleepers, "they preserve the goal in the future that every human being is to see a hidden divine essence in every other human being.[5]

When the human spirit becomes hardened in earthbound intellect, this divine spirit becomes less effective. One antidote is to preserve a childlike nature within. The angelic nature is closest to the child, and as the child grows into an adult this spirit gradually withdraws and transfers its activity to the periphery of life, bringing wisdom and clarity only indirectly to meet the inner spirit, sometimes just giving hints or stimulation. These free opportunities for growth can be used or not. These moments can come through a remark, a line from a book, or a thought working in a moment of transition. Jung referred to these moments as "synchronicity," something symbolic of our inner world that is reflected in the outer world. For example, one summer night a friend was sitting with her husband on their back deck looking at the stars and discussing the challenges they had experienced in their relationship with a Native American elder they knew. This elder belongs to the Bear Clan. At that moment they heard a large crash, and their dog started barking. When the woman walked to the end of the deck and turned on the porch light, there, ten feet away, stood a huge black bear. This is a moment of synchronicity. The opportunity for growth comes in asking the question, What is the meaning in this for me?

Another clue to this angelic nature lies in noticing what happens during those times when one is prevented from doing something: The angel "waits to see what man will start to do with his freedom ... the angel waits. The ability to have patience and forbearance is the virtue of the angels; their growth in divine light is directly connected to the proving of such loyalty, such faithfulness."[6] When we are challenged, tested, overwhelmed, it is especially difficult to create the space for faithfulness, a quality that enables us to let go and trust the unseen or, as that great rationalist Socrates called it, the "higher Thou" to work in our daily lives. For many teachers who are asked to be attentive and present every minute of the day, holding, inspiring, and directing a group of children, letting go is not part of the job description. The demands of teaching require confidence and projection of self. Most experienced teachers, in fact, radiate a sense of authority that serves the children well. (Whether this is always best for parent/teacher interactions will be considered later.) Yet this daily practice of classroom leadership, being "on" all the time, can be the opposite spiritual practice from letting go with the childlike nature of the angelic. The personal spiritual practice of the teacher must then take up the balance—the receptive, opening attitude that can allow for an instreaming of new substance from that which is greater than oneself, what Zen Buddhists refer to as the Void and Chinese philosophers name the Tao.[7] A personal spiritual practice may not be a requirement for a teaching job in most schools, but in terms of renewal, it is a necessity.

One might say that in the classroom, the teacher becomes greater or the focal point, but in personal spiritual practice, the teacher must decrease and become the lesser. Although students, especially in elementary school, may rightly see the teacher as the fount of wisdom, sharing the likes of Pythagoras and Buddha, the human being standing in the classroom as the teacher most likely is less developed inwardly. If this contrast is conscious, it can lead to healthy humility. The sense that "I am not as great as that which I am allowed to teach" can lead to a spiritual path that promotes integration and renewal. One can become more aware of the two companions, both the shadow and the angel, that accompany us through life. As Psalm 91 says: "For he shall give his angels charge over thee, to keep thee in all thy ways."

The Spark of Life

In legend, Prometheus is the friend of humankind who defies Zeus and steals fire from the heavens and brings it back in a fennel stalk to give to human beings. His punishment from the gods is to be forever chained to a rock in the Caucasus, where an eagle tears out his liver again and again each time that it grows back. The Greek playwright Aeschylus adds this detail of the story: Prometheus knows that if Zeus has a child with the nymph Thetis, their son will be stronger than Zeus and eventually will overthrow him. Prometheus accepts his torture on the rock rather than reveal this secret to the god, because in not revealing it, he has power over Zeus. Thus he is forever chained and suffering, yet confident of his ultimate victory.[8]

This Greek legend can help us understand the battle for personal and professional renewal. First we have the liver, which is the physical seat of life forces. In terms of anthroposophy, Steiner suggests that this life force, or the desire of all things to grow, is something we share not only with animals but also with the plant kingdom. In the story of Prometheus, the liver continually grows back, just as the life forces work daily to replenish and renew the human body. Countering this dynamic, however, we find the eagle or vulture that repeatedly devours the liver while Prometheus is chained to the rock. For native peoples the eagle flies closest to Grandfather Sun and is therefore a symbol of clarity and illumination. Like the eagle flying close to the illuminating rays of the Sun, humans have an eagle-like quality called "consciousness," which is fed by the innate life forces. Thus, there is a kind of ongoing battle between the forces of life and the consciousness that feeds upon them.

Here again we see the theme of balance in the journey for renewal. In our daily lives, we work with both these elements. In that we work rhythmically, eat nourishing food, sleep well, and experience the arts, we are able to sustain our life forces. Gardening and working with nature, in particular, can enhance this kind of health. As Steiner suggested, the plant world is the clearest example of life forces at work. Plants, trees, and flowers grow and in this display the laws of growth. As humans, we also have consciousness. We think about our tasks, solve problems, engage in issues, prepare for teaching, and reflect upon our experiences. It is our exercise of consciousness that makes us distinctly human, able to distinguish between good and evil, right and wrong. Through our consciousness, we are awake to the world and the Inner Self. Yet in exercising this freedom, we use life forces that otherwise would be used for physical health. Thus, there are two extremes: We can use too little consciousness and become "couch potatoes," responding minimally to outer stimuli and living more like a vegetable than a person. Or we can become so awake and conscious, live so strongly in thinking, that we become over-extended in more ways than one. Every time we use our consciousness, we consume life forces that need to be replenished.

In traditional Chinese medicine, human equilibrium is seen not only in the balance of body, mind, and spirit but also in the balance between the person and the social realm. The hope is that one can achieve balance by finding equilibrium between using energy and storing it. Each task requires a certain amount of energy, and the self-aware person will expend only the energy needed for a particular task. The "yang" of active dispersing and the "yin" for storing and containing needs to be artfully offset. The five elements—water, wood, fire, earth, and metal—represent the five phases of development, which are accomplished in one way or another in any living system. The goal is to balance the five forms of energy in daily living.[9]

On a practical level there are things we can do to achieve balance. For instance, after a long meeting in which people are talking and living in the world of ideas, it is helpful to find a counterbalancing activity, such as walking in nature, painting with watercolors, making music, or simply enjoying quiet time and rest. Turning inward, communing with nature, working artistically, and spending quiet time tend to replenish and draw life forces together, while meetings, conversation, outer activity, and the press of daily living tend to disperse them.

One can become increasingly sensitive to this Promethean dynamic by constantly asking the question: When am I consuming, and when am I replenishing? If a teacher like Sarah, or any of us, can learn to listen to this question, it is possible to forestall serious illnesses, for most imbalances occur first on the inner level before they manifest in the body. How many of us, like Sarah, have gone through a challenging or stressful personal time only to come down suddenly with a terrible cold or flu that forces us to stop, rest, and reflect? The issue of replenishment is especially important for human beings today. Unlike other life forms, for us physical renewal does not come automatically. For instance, if you cut down a sapling, it often will grow again within a short time. When a limb is severed from a tree, sap will flow freely—a physical manifestation of life forces. Then the limb will try to grow back. In plants, tremendous healing forces are activated when an injury occurs. The life forces of the plant express increased activity when the physical is injured.

Among indigenous peoples the world over, the shaman or medicine man/woman uses plants for their healing powers. In addition, the shaman travels into the realm of the intuitive, the world of dreams and the emotions—usually by entering a trance using drums and chants. In this realm the shaman can speak with the spirit of the plant or meet the spirit of the person who is ill. The final step in this kind of healing is for the person who is ill to perform a symbolic act. Among the Navajo people there is an entire ceremony called the Enemy Way, in which a soldier who has been in battle and killed other human beings must engage in days of singing, prayers, and offerings in the effort to return to harmony. This type of symbolic act has a practical aspect, in that it brings the cause of the illness to the consciousness of the person being healed. This idea is not so far-fetched. How many of us have lit candles, used rosary beads, or knelt in prayer for those who are ill or suffering?

Just as the shaman uses plants and the emotional and intuitive aspects of human life and conscious behavior to heal, so, too, does Steiner connect these aspects of life to healing. In anthroposophy Steiner suggests that initially there is the physical world of rocks and stones. Then there is the world of plants, which demonstrates the life force, or the quality of growth. Next, as we saw in Sarah's story, there is what Steiner terms the "emotional" or sensate body or realm. Steiner pointed out that in addition to the life force, animals have a consciousness realm as well. As any animal lover knows, animals are able to experience some of our emotions, our joy, excitement, and pain. This type of consciousness is less developed than in humans; animals are not able to work with these experiences, yet they have a level of consciousness not seen in plants. Thus, the life force of the animal reacts correspondingly less effectively to an external injury.

Although lower animal forms, such as the triton, can grow back an amputated organ and a slightly higher form, such as the crab, can heal over time by repeatedly casting off its shell, a dog or a cat cannot grow back a leg. The healing energies of the life forces have to make greater efforts to assert themselves the higher one goes in the animal kingdom. This stems from the type of connection between the physical nature and the life force. In the triton, the connection between the physical nature and the life force is quite loose; thus the organ can be regenerated easily. In the higher animals and in humans, however, the connection between the life force and the physical nature is much more intimate, and physical stress or injury is imposed not only on our physical being but also on that part of our nature that carries the unseen force of life.

Here we come to a crucial point: The emotional and sensory nature, the conscious life of feelings and emotions, exposes the human being much more to the influences of the outside world, and this exposure holds sway over the life force, which then has to work harder to heal. Impressions of the outer world make an imprint on our emotions, which affects the mobility of the life force, which is then less free to heal the physical. These relationships of life force and emotions, according to Steiner, have many implications for our personal and professional development. If a person leads a dissolute life, it will make an impression on the emotional realm, which in turn influences the life force. What we do influences not only our friends and community but also our inner life of consciousness. In turn, what we hold in our consciousness affects the health of our life forces. Thus, we can see that we alter our life forces depending upon the kind of inner and outer lives we lead.

If this idea seems too abstract, try a simple exercise: Try to experience the influence of negative versus positive thoughts on your being for a few days. For a day or so, let your consciousness be filled with negative thoughts. See how you feel as you carry them around. You may be less energetic, even lethargic. Then try to erase negative thoughts when they arise and continually replace them with positive thoughts—the glass half full instead of half empty. See how you respond. After a few days of working on seeing the positive, you may be truly more buoyant, enthusiastic, energetic. Our thought life (consciousness) influences our regeneration.

The mythic story of Prometheus and the dynamic of consuming and replenishing give us a symbol for our own renewal as we experience our day-to-day struggles. How we personally regenerate influences the health of our schools. Overextended, wrung out, overly-busy parents and teachers sap the life forces from the children and tend to experience more conflict with other adults. Healthy, vibrant, centered teachers and parents help create a culture of respect, trust, and goodwill. Much that either works or does not work in our schools is influenced to a great degree by the basics of personal health. I once knew a teacher who was struggling on all fronts, with classroom management, with colleagues, and with parents. It seemed to me that she would soon leave teaching. Much to my delight, upon returning to her school a few years later, I found a thriving, successful teacher. What had happened? A brief conversation revealed that she had found someone new in her life, had begun a routine of regular exercise, and had given herself permission to try new ideas in her classroom. She was flourishing, and the collegial problems were gone. Her health had made the school a better place. Rather than always looking to outside solutions (conflict resolution, strategic planning, trust-building retreats), much could be achieved if people just took themselves in hand.

Technology and Faith

> The complexity of external life will steadily increase and however many activities are taken over from human beings in the future by machines, there can be very few lives of happiness in this present incarnation unless conditions quite different from those now prevailing are brought about.
>
> —Rudolf Steiner[10]

Ten years ago, my early morning routine at the office included opening mail, responding to phone messages, and clearing the desk for my first appointments of the day. This took about an hour and sometimes even included time to answer a few inquiries. Then we all began to receive voice mail, and suddenly there were all sorts of new possibilities for obtaining, storing, sharing, and transferring phone calls. My morning routine was lengthened considerably. With the fax, I found that more people were communicating more frequently, and the pace of life picked up. Then, in the last years of the twentieth century, e-mail was available to all of us in offices. Suddenly a whole host of communications began to occur, some of which seemed to have nothing to do with me. I was "spammed" by unknown organizations and individuals, copied by colleagues, and inundated with e-mail attachments. Snail mail was still arriving, my voice mail was full every few hours, and the e-mail "pinged" me continually.

Recently I made an inventory of my day at the office, ten years later. I found that most of my day was now consumed by these various forms of communication. In some cases, such as reading student journals, there was a sense of working with real content, but in many instances, I found myself responding, responding, and responding. Looking at my inner life while doing so, I discovered that I was spending a good part of the day in a mild state of annoyance. Beneath the surface, I kept wishing, "Enough already, I hope no one else calls or sends me an e-mail." The antisocial part of me was churning, and I felt a constant sense of restlessness.

It was a shock to realize that despite my spiritual practice at other times in the day, my consciousness was being shaped by technology. It had taken hold of me. Every time I started to have a real thought, the phone would ring, the console light would flash, and the e-mail would ping. If left to its own devices, my consciousness would become like a giant octopus, tentacles churning in a murky sea of too much communication. Then I started to look at the content of the communication and found that much was of a superficial nature. Students and colleagues asked me questions in a manner that they never would in person. My e-mail responses were so brief that they occasionally bordered on the impolite. For the most part, I was dealing with ideas divorced from human beings. If left to its natural course, my life could become one long series of cartoons without Disney's animation. This could lead to a feeling of subtle dissatisfaction, which would spill over into interpersonal relations. After hours of dealing with "cartoon ideas," I had to struggle to be warm and exercise basic courtesy. It took more work just to be human!

As a result of these and other observations about the influence of technology in my life, I made a few New Millennium resolutions. I decided both to increase and to decrease aspects of my life. I limited the amount of time spent on fears of unmet expectations, fears of failing to "comply" dutifully with the demands of the modern workplace, fears of feeling incomplete and inattentive. Fear is a corrosive emotion that can eat away gradually at the soul, causing a kind of hollowness that immobilizes and holds a person back from making the changes needed in life. I restricted e-mail and nonessential phone conversations and channeled communication that needed more "humanity" toward the phone rather than e-mail. If necessary, I would leave the office at the end of the day without responding to all my messages, and I would realize that I had not failed in my life's work. I also increased the number of face-to-face meetings with students whenever possible, either by sitting in the office or by taking a walk. In fact, walking seems really to help the flow of conversation and assist both people in flexibility of thought. I resolved to carve out time for in-depth conversation with a friend or colleague, rather than just always handling business. And I affirmed the difference between thinking and technology-driven responses, knowing that my clarity would help maintain inner health.

There is a benefit to technology, one that is evident as I write this book. Editing, moving paragraphs, and adding footnotes once took hours of retyping when I was in college. Now I am able to make changes more easily and exercise greater flexibility in thinking as a result. Yet the call to new consciousness is greater. For instance, I found that my hand, arm, and shoulder muscles often experienced subtle aches after an hour or two at the keyboard. After longer periods, my back would require physical therapy. Now I have turned things around with the addition of various gadgets, such as an extended keyboard, lap pad, and proper lighting. Also, I take breaks when I need them, rather than just when it is possible to do so.

All this plays into the quality of human interactions and the challenges to renewal in our schools. How are parents and teachers spending their time each day? If a parent is living in the world of e-commerce for hours on end and then meets with a teacher for a conference, you can bet his or her daily activities will influence the human exchange. Likewise, if teachers spend increasing amounts of time monitoring their e-mail and working online, how will they be with their students?

The whole issue is far subtler than these reflections indicate. Anything mechanized tends to weaken life forces and harden consciousness. Someone forced to type all day long, especially in a noncreative mode, will feel a decrease in vitality, both physically and in the inner life. Dealing with a mechanized medium without counterbalancing activities can lead to ill health. But when such work is combined with superficiality of content, the results are more severe. To use an image, the human being can become like a great eggshell, brittle on the outside and devoid of much yolk. Externalization leads to hollowness. The inner journey can suffer. If the reader can identify with at least some of what has been described, the real question then can arise: What can parents and teachers do to counteract externalization?

The work of the soul must grow to keep pace with external demands. The soul of the human being can be enlivened, vitalized, and redirected to overcome the damaging influences of our materialistic culture. One way to do this, though most people do not see it as *modern*, is through the simple yet profound act called *faith*. Faith is that sense of trust that leaves the door open for change, whereas cynicism closes it. Although one perhaps cannot trust a human being totally, if one did not have faith that there is the capacity for love, one would find little reason to bother, to move on, and to grow. When a human being cultivates faith, it has a life-giving influence on the soul whereas skepticism does the opposite—it dries up and hardens the soul. Life today has become ever more complicated. We cannot avoid the changes of our times. We do have a choice; we have the ability to balance external culture through a deepened inner life.

Faith, regardless of affiliation with a church, can awaken the human soul. One might see it as the lending of the inner self to something higher, inexplicable, and greater than the things of the world. Grandmother Twylah Nitsch, a Seneca elder, uses a medicine wheel in which Faith and Trust sit in the place of the south, while directly across, in the north, sit Wisdom and Gratitude. She believes that practicing faith and trust in our lives leads to wisdom.[11] External society often seeks to make us content with things that can be possessed; faith leads us beyond. Faith leads, and our inner self is nourished through devotion.

Devotion is the path of most teachers. They work for low wages and little prestige. More and more of society's challenges are thrust upon the schools, especially our public schools. Whenever there is a new concern or media sensation, legislators pass a law mandating changes in curriculum, often without the information or understanding of how to implement the new mandate. Teachers are asked to include more each year, but nobody ever seems to think of removing any of the previous mandates. Often, what the state deems important runs counter to what the teachers find that their students need. Yet they continue teaching, out of love of their students and the chance to make a difference. This is devotion.

Beyond externals, this attitude of the dedicated teacher serves to nourish the soul in ways that cannot be underestimated. The soul is nurtured by being devoted to something bigger than it is, something it can strive for in the search for oneness. Devotion in the soul is like a cup that beholds and nurtures the growing content within. When devotion is engaged, there is a growing inner fullness that strengthens the desire to live and participate in the world, no matter how great the challenges might be. Devotion gives the teacher or parent the inner fire to get up each morning and go at it again. When one is truly devoted to a person or a task, one can carry almost anything. The soul is bigger than life. It is the source of continual rejuvenation.

This strengthening of the inner life also affects the state of our physical health, our social interactions, and our ability to do what is asked of us. Particularly in and around schools, people are called upon to make sacrifices, to give and volunteer beyond the call of duty. Yet when parents and teachers repeatedly sacrifice without the inner substance out of which to give, burnout results. People like to sacrifice; it gives pleasure, and the rewards are many. But there cannot be a sacrifice of lasting value unless one has the strength to give. We cannot look to technology to give us the needed inner resources. Individuals must be something before they can give productively. The renewal of our schools depends upon the self-realization and inner vitality of the human beings devoting themselves to the cause of education. To prevent egotism of the worst kind, it is essential that the adults in and around a school practice what they expect of the children, namely, self-development and personal change.

Balance

Once we confront the dual nature in ourselves, the black and green of Elegba, the question arises, How do we come into balance with this duality? How does one carry this spiritual practice of balancing one's inner life with the outer realities of the day-to-day life of the teacher? Here are the stories of two teachers and their very different experiences. In reading these stories, we see how these two people dealt with the need for balance in themselves, their classrooms, and their schools.

A first-year teacher called me recently. He wanted to check in, share the news and experiences of the first few months of teaching. Condensed somewhat, this is what he said: "My teaching is going well. I feel the group has come together, even though several new children have joined the class. There are more boys than there are girls, and the age span is wider than I had expected, but they seem to be working well. After several weeks of intermittent minor illness, I am recovering and beginning to find a rhythm for preparation. Of course, there is never enough time, but gradually I am learning to focus on the essential. I am also happy with my colleagues, and I am getting to know the parents.

"Within weeks I was asked to join two committees. I declined one, but now I am in a quandary. As I look around the faculty, it seems that a few people are doing most of the work. They are experienced teachers, but they are carrying too heavy a load. These few are called upon for chairing meetings and addressing administrative work such as hiring, interviewing, and correspondence, and they also are expected to speak at public events and somehow fit in time for mentoring the three other new teachers and me. When I say no to a committee or task, it simply heaps more work on these few. If they burn out, what will happen to the school? Yet if I say yes to the many needs, will I not eventually become just like them? What should I do?"

I responded by talking about biography—not his per se, but the biography of a relationship to a school. As a first-year teacher, he naturally saw everything from that perspective, and the issue of the shared administrative responsibility of a Waldorf teacher was a present dilemma. I suggested that he look at his role over a three-, five-, or eight-year time span. As his teaching became more secure, he could contribute more and more to the general life of the school. In the meantime, he should not under-estimate the importance of doing small things: for example, spontaneously offering to take a colleague's recess or lunch supervision, pitching in when that colleague is moving furniture or setting up props for a play. He could do jobs that do not involve heavy responsibility but could lessen the load of those who carry the school in leadership capacities. "Followership" can be as important to a school as leadership. And, finally, I advised him to remember that no matter what stage of one's school biography one is in, a person can help carry his or her colleagues through active, inner support. Picturing them before sleep, seeing them as successful in one's mind's eye, and giving them a vote of confidence will stream out as positive support in your attitude and intentions.

As I spent time on the phone with this particular teacher, I realized how fortunate he was to have the classroom work well in hand and at least have access to mentorship. This was not the case with another first-year teacher, who shared his anguished point of view with me in a letter. One always has to remember in hearing such an account that this is his perspective on the experience, which nevertheless can help us understand the urgency of school renewal. This was his story:

"I had a problem during my first teaching job, which forced me to resign. Though the problem was quite involved, I will describe as briefly as I can what happened, in the hope that others may be helped toward avoiding a similar situation. I began teaching first grade in an established Waldorf school in September 1999. I had a written mentorship agreement with a teacher who had been teaching for twenty-six years. The agreement stated, among other things, that she would come into my classroom 'six to nine days' to assess, 'troubleshoot,' and otherwise help and advise me with specific suggestions stemming out of her observations of my class and me. The problems that arose were as follows:

"Though I repeatedly asked her during the first month of school to come in and observe, per our agreement, my mentor, for whatever reason, refused to do so. In retrospect, I think this was partly because she was involved with her own class to such a degree that she inadvertently shut the door on her responsibility to me and was not able to face up to the fact that I was thereby denied crucial support. At any rate, because of my own inexperience, my six-year-olds were too loud and out of control at times, and my mentor began complaining about it to the school administrators and heads of faculty without telling me she was doing so. We shared the top floor, so if the children were loud, she would hear it. Instead of feeling supported, therefore, I began to feel more and more isolated without really knowing why, because nothing had been said to me or addressed in a forthright manner.

"This strange give-and-take continued until the fifth week, when someone from another school was sent to my classroom to do what my mentor was not able to do. I was very grateful, and I learned a great deal from his observations and suggestions. However, once again without my being apprised of it, this new teacher went to the heads of the school with a written assessment that was more of an indictment and judgment against me. It was deliberated over and became the main basis for my dismissal, though I was under the impression he had been there to support me and help me become a better teacher. Every new teacher needs this support, even if it is only moral support, and I thought I was finally receiving what I had most needed, had asked for often, and had thought I was assured of getting via my mentor agreement. I later found out how wrong I was.

"As it turned out, these two teachers were very good and longtime friends and associates who had worked together in this very school nine or ten years earlier. The second teacher was pressured or chose to resign at that time for political/collegial reasons. I do not think they were consciously trying to antagonize my position, but I think more was communicated between them because of their past associations than they were aware of.

"Anyway, his assessment of my classroom teaching was given to the college of teachers without my knowing about it or being given a copy, and on the basis of that assessment the school decided to fire me. At this point I still had heard nothing about any of this! Later, when I read his assessment, I found it to be completely inconsistent; most of his conclusions were belied by his own observations! Be that as it may, the decision to let me go came in the eighth week at the college meeting; by the following Sunday I still hadn't been told anything. My intuition, however, and a sense of what was going on had become acute. With my brother called in as a witness, I had a meeting with the faculty chair and college chair. I told them I felt so unsupported by the school, yet in such an unspoken way that it seemed they were ready to fire me and that I felt so besieged that I could not do my job properly and was ready to resign.

"They said that I was right and that they had decided to let me go the previous Thursday. At this point I told them that my mentor had never come in to help me, as she had agreed. For this reason, of which the college was unaware, they said they would rescind their decision to dismiss me and discuss it again in this new light. They also told me that they had based my dismissal on the second teacher's assessment, which I still knew nothing about and had not seen. I said I should already have received a copy of it, and I wanted to see one as soon as possible.

"Two days later, after finally receiving the assessment, I was very angry and deeply disappointed, because I knew that I could no longer work under such conditions and ways of thinking and saw no choice but to resign. Before their college meeting to discuss my dismissal a second time, I informed the chairpersons of my decision. We set up a meeting for the day after that college meeting to discuss a time frame for my departure. At this last meeting, one of them said: 'It is all very well that you think you had a mentorship agreement with the school, but the only agreement you ever had with us is the school contract.' I was incredulous and asked her if she thought that I had made it up. She said, 'You keep mentioning it, but we've never seen it.' At this I was astounded. I showed them the agreement, and the three of them were dumbfounded. I could see that they were as aghast as I was that none of them knew anything about it whatsoever, let alone had a copy. They didn't even know who had written it. I pointed out that as my employers, who had discussed all this with me back in June 1999, they should have written it. I said that it was unforgivable, unconscionable, and unprofessional in the extreme that such a thing could happen.

"It turned out that my mentor had written the agreement. No doubt she was asked to do so by the school, but they had never received a copy of it, or they had lost it, and no one ever followed up on it. For a beginning teacher, however, it is an extremely important document. It never occurred to me that I should check to make sure the school had a copy of it. Also, one must make sure that such an agreement is very clear and specific in the terms and dates of its implementation. Mine said 'six to nine days' of observation, but it did not say when these days would be. I expected that they would be sooner rather than later, because as a new teacher I knew I would need mentoring in the beginning. The school's tendency was later rather than sooner.

"At the end of that last meeting, I said I would stay on for as long as it took them to find a new teacher but that I knew definitively that by resigning I had done the only thing I could have done under the circumstances. I enjoined them to scrutinize and improve upon the school's performance in this regard, as it was bordering on ludicrous and very destructive to me. They were grateful for and accepted my words, and two of them thanked me sincerely. I could see they felt bad about what had happened. Two weeks later, the day before Thanksgiving, I taught my last class."

Knowing the teachers in these two stories and their colleagues, I can say unequivocally that they are good people. They meet weekly, share readings of high social ideals, and value community. Yet because of the demands of school life and interpersonal dynamics, what becomes evident through both these stories is a group of overextended individuals. They all suffer from the breakdown in communication, group dynamics, leadership, and mentorship, but the sense of being overwhelmed is so great that no one seems to be able to rise above it all. Must this be?

It is not just the teachers who are searching for balance. Many parents also put in long hours at work, race from one chauffeuring assignment to another, have little time for family, and still feel constantly guilty because the school seems always to need volunteers. As one parent in a Waldorf school said to me recently: "We work hard to meet the tuition payments, yet the school continually hosts events for which we have to pay an entrance fee, make multiple phone calls, and bake cookies."

Since the organization of a Waldorf School requires the full participation of teachers and parents, the problems of finding balance are particularly acute. Everyone involved in any kind of school community can identify with one aspect or another of these two stories of well-meaning individuals who are overextended. So a central question for school renewal is, How can a teacher, or any adult involved in a school community, find balance in living? I asked this question with slightly different wording in a survey of experienced Waldorf teachers: "In striving to maintain a balance between health, family, and teaching/administration, what tips can you pass on to colleagues preparing to join a Waldorf school?"

The answers cover many of the areas of deepest concern to the majority of teachers. It is always helpful to hear the words of one's colleagues in their struggles to find the balance we all seek. Here are some examples:

• Don't become a Waldorf teacher if you wish for this balance. The system is not set up to support a balance, and there are no tips that can change the basic math of the fifty-five to seventy hours or longer workweek and the drain this causes on health, family, and a personal life. That being said, I do have a few tips that can help a bit:

• Use an answering machine, preferably on a separate phone line, for school calls. Tell parents in your class they are likely to get the machine when they call and that you prefer to return calls during working hours. Turn off the ringer on your phone so that the calls do not interrupt your personal life. Check the messages each evening and return emergency calls only. Insist that you have office space with a phone to return calls during the day. The larger your class is, the more you will need a system like this. Parents in my class call me more on this system, because they know they are not disturbing me.

• Most Waldorf schools would be judged by psychologists as having a poor understanding of boundaries between the personal and professional life. It is easy to feel as if one is always at work. Faculties should share information about when they will or will not accept work calls from each other. There should be a limit on the number of evening and weekend events one is expected to attend.

• Teachers, board members, and parents need to work together to change the basic math of a teacher's job. Is there a reason for the long workweek? In a pioneering school, there usually is a reason for this high level of commitment. In an established school, this level of commitment is counterproductive, since it drains health, stresses marriages and parent-child relationships, and does not support creativity in teaching. The American family has changed significantly in the past ten to fifteen years so that, more and more, both spouses work full-time. At one time, a typical family had one adult in the workplace for forty hours a week. Now many families, not just Waldorf teachers, devote 100–150 hours per week to the workplace. The impact on children is significant. As a teacher, I see that the children with overcommitted parents are the most emotionally fragile. Waldorf schools should be workplace leaders in supporting a healthy family life.

• The key to this change is to provide more preparation time at school. Teachers need offices, telephones, computers, library resources, and time to be in their offices. The Waldorf curriculum demands a high level of preparation, but Waldorf schools do nothing to support teachers to do preparation during the normal workday. This also leads to a "quality control" problem. The teacher with an at-home spouse and few home or child-care responsibilities can devote more evening or weekend time than a single parent can, for instance. So different classes in the same school receive different levels of teacher attention based on the personal commitment of the teacher. Supporting teacher preparation would bring a more uniform quality to teaching.

Of the eighty-odd responses, at least one-third reiterated the need for balance by a statement similar to this one: "Learn to say no and set limits."

Learning to say no, setting boundaries and limits, clearly is an important goal for Waldorf teachers and for everyone who works in a serving profession. In looking for balance, however, we must take care that the use of the term "boundary" does not become an excuse for not attending, not participating, and in general letting others do the work one should do oneself. One has to maintain a balance between self-centeredness and going beyond one's limits. As in the first response cited, one of the major areas of concern was the home and one's own children. The experience of these Waldorf teachers is that their homes need to be a haven and that the support of one's spouse and children is necessary. This is indicated in the detailed response of the first teacher and of the additional comments of many teachers represented by this one: "If you have children, don't neglect them. Keep being their parent. They will reward you in the end."

Setting limits, learning to say no, leads to the consideration of how to achieve that balance in work, which is truly a calling for many people. The following comments are just a few that reflect this need:

> • If people are having a hard time maintaining a balance while in training [Waldorf Teacher Training], they should really examine themselves and how they organize their time and energy, because demands very likely will be even higher once they're teaching. Common-sense habits like adequate sleep, diet, and exercise are critical, as is some sort of inner path of development and artistic life away from school/ teaching activity. Building in time for review and reflection

opens a door for change and growth rather than staying overly busy all the time.

• In an initiative school, it was very difficult to maintain a balance, because the parents often see the teacher as the authority on everything and therefore believe the teacher is the best person to get the word about the school out into the world. Therefore, building enrollment and getting involved on committees and community events often can take precedence over teaching and everything else. I found that developing close connections with mentor teachers and other teachers in the area was the best support.

Other helpful ideas for keeping a balance in school life and personal life included the constant admonition to get enough sleep and other practical suggestions, such as these:

• If parents do shiatsu, massage, cranial therapy, teachers need work often. Bartering possible? Set up regular sessions at the school.

• Take hot baths. Organize a yoga instructor to teach a class during weekends at your school. Stop drinking coffee. Carry Rescue Remedy at all times. Turn off the phone from dinner through your child's bedtime. Let go one day of the weekend. Go to sleep by 9:00 p.m. Park far away and walk to school.

• Actively cultivate a life and interests separate from the school life/community.

Still other suggestions focused on ways to work in the classroom and with the children:

• Strive to "breathe" in your life the way you strive to have your lessons breathe.

• Give yourself half the year to find your rhythm before taking on extra committee work.

• Be very organized in your files, daily calendar, etc.

• I find that the evening and morning meditations on the kids go much further than the small effort I put into them. I also take a moment, maybe even sixty seconds or more, before the morning verse when we all strive to become quiet inwardly.

• Create and maintain a network of other Waldorf teachers at your grade level or above. Refer to your class as "my students," not "my children."

• Make sure you have a mentor to help you through the first year.

• Love the children and their families.

Finally, in the area of balance between the teacher and the school the following suggestions were given:

• Is your school board focused on clear objectives? Does the board have a system of rotating in new board members? Does your school have a plan for funding sabbaticals and making salaries reasonable?

• Hire a person who is trained in school administration and qualified to handle the daily operations. This would relieve a great deal of strife.

• Join a union.

• Delegate to class parents all organizing of outside activities.

• Rotate Open House responsibilities.

• Have faculty goals for pedagogical study and share ideas as part of faculty meetings; combine meetings when possible (parent council 6–7, class meeting 7–8:30).

• Find a balance between listening to parents and giving them control.

And, last, the words of this teacher remind us of our primary focus:

> • Be realistic with expectations. You're only human. The children will be fine in spite of your mistakes. Try to ignore the parents and get on with the children. Take cues from Steiner and what the children need.

I am sure that many of you reading this book can relate to these words of your fellow teachers. The themes raised in this survey are the content of most of this book: renewal through spiritual practice, establishing boundaries, setting priorities, organizing preparation time, learning to say no, finding helpful administrative structures, learning to work with others, and valuing personal as well as professional time.

One major source of teacher stress not discussed much elsewhere has to do with parenting. What is not carried at home often spills over into the school. Teachers end up doing much more than teaching, thus contributing to the burdens carried by those at school and again creating the potential for imbalance. The biggest problem in parenting today can be described in one word: desertion. Parents often simply are not there. I recently heard that one family set itself the goal of eating at least one meal per week together. Per *week*! The rest of the time, the children fended for themselves, opening the fridge at all times of the day, eating when hungry, and acting like little individuals and not part of a social unit. Parents today are so busy with work and other responsibilities that little time is left for sharing news, homework, recreation, or bedtime stories. I have seen a harassed mother trying to read to a three-year old in the checkout line at the supermarket! Above all, parents are often just not there, physically and emotionally.

When parents are present, they frequently treat their children as they would a spouse or a partner, having adult-like conversations and offering choices beyond the scope of the child. This may be a simple matter of asking, "Should we have fish or chicken tonight?" Or it might be more fundamental, such as "Do you want to go to camp today?" My mother once observed a neighbor's six-year-old child waiting for the bus in a T-shirt. The temperature on that February day was 20 degrees Fahrenheit. Later that day, when she met the mother, she voiced her concern. The mother replied, "Yes, he does have a winter coat, but he decided that he would wear his T-shirt today. He makes all his own decisions. And when it is a family matter, we take a vote." Democracy for six-year-olds!

The effect of giving children too many choices before they have the capacity to exercise judgment is to paralyze the inner life, weaken the life forces that are needed for growth, and create little grownups with nervous disorders and other dubious benefits of adulthood. A day filled with short-term, meaningless choices—"Do you want raspberry or strawberry yogurt today?"—can have a profound effect on the sleep life of our children. An uncertain world of daytime choices can lead to restlessness in sleep. I have seen many children come to school tired not because they had not slept enough, but because the quality of their sleep was poor. Of course, their sleep interruptions add to the stress of their parents! The role of sleep is so important to school renewal or renewal of any kind that I have devoted an entire chapter to it later in this book. Ironically, the tendency to present too many choices to children often is combined with overindulgence. Perhaps out of guilt because there is little quality time together or because of their own childhood experiences, parents spoil their children. They wait on them at home, require few chores, and say things without following up with consequences. Words then become meaningless, and children get the message that adults are to be tolerated at best and ignored if need be.

All this then falls into the lap of teachers. By definition, they are authority figures who need to use speech as a tool of the trade. Yet increasingly teachers find that their students cannot listen, have little respect for authority, and have been indulged to the point of being willful. But most of all, I feel that teachers struggle with social needs that are enormous, given the absence of family life. The classroom then becomes the only place where sharing, conversing, learning work habits, and conflict resolution are practiced. Teachers in inner cities and poor rural districts sometimes have to feed and clothe their students. In short, the role of teachers has expanded and that of parents has diminished. This lack of balance needs to be addressed as a community issue, in order for parents and teachers to be able to support one another.

For the teacher like Sarah who is striving to achieve balance, one needs to begin the journey for renewal with oneself, to find one's inner center, a place of authorship, creativity, certainty. You can see how matters stand with a parent or teacher by observing his or her interactions with the children and asking the question, Is this person working out of that center or more from the periphery? Is he or she present and aware or distracted and unfocused? Once teachers have made the commitment to work on themselves, they can begin to look at the imbalances that arise in their interactions with the students and school. If we can give our children a true experience of authority, they will grow up with confidence and optimism. I long to hear parents say, "I have packed your lunch with a cheese sandwich, apple, juice, and strawberry yogurt. This is what I want you to have for lunch today." If there is a big fuss, or if the child refuses to eat what has been so lovingly prepared, let him go without. There is not much danger in experiencing a bit of hunger once in a while, and strawberry yogurt tastes ever so good with a real appetite.

Most important of all is the *soul food* that the parent or teacher gives the child, with that sense of inner certainty and decisiveness. Children who experience authority that is exercised out of love will gain the ability to make real choices when they are older, choices that come from the wellspring of a rich inner life not just the nervous energy of sensory stimulation. When teachers and parents find their inner equilibrium, consult their inner compass and not their young children, and exercise rightful decision making for those in their care, schools will exude vitality and enthusiasm for life.

4

LOOKING IN THE MIRROR

The Devil with the Three Golden Hairs

*There was once a poor woman who gave birth to a little son;
and as he came into the world with a caul on, it was predicted that
in his fourteenth year he would have the King's daughter for his
wife....*

*The King, who had a bad heart, and was angry about the
prophecy, went to the parents ... and offered them a large amount of
gold for it....*

*The King put it in a box and rode away with it until he came
to a deep piece of water; then he threw the box into it and thought:
"I have freed my daughter from her undesired suitor."*

*The box, however, did not sink, but floated like a boat, and not
a drop of water made its way into it. And it floated to within two
miles of the King's chief city, where there was a mill, and it came to
a halt at the mill-dam. A miller's boy, who by good luck was standing there, noticed it and pulled it out with a hook, thinking that he
had found a great treasure, but when he opened it there lay a pretty
boy inside, quite fresh and lively. He took him to the miller and his
wife, and as they had no children they were glad and said: "God has
given him to us." They took great care of the foundling, and he grew
up in all goodness.*[12]

There is much wisdom captured in this story, as with other
fairy tales passed on from early times, when human beings were

related more closely to the world of myth. Although other stories could be used, I have found this one particularly helpful in terms of understanding personal renewal. A child cast adrift is a theme echoed in mythology, from Moses to Romulus and Remus, and it speaks of a special soul that is freed of heredity and destined for greatness. Carried by the life forces of the flowing water, such children are brought to the right shore by the waves and wind of destiny. Most teachers are like the miller and his wife, glad to take the child in and provide for him temporarily while he is in their care. But this is a special child, one who stands for the truly human and for the heart that is protected from outer challenges, symbolized by the fact that "not a drop of water" enters the box. The King, in contrast, has the outer authority, but his heart is eclipsed and no longer true. The foundling counters that which is incomplete in the outer world.

Fourteen is a crucial age, and at that time in the foundling's biography, the King with an evil heart once again tries to intervene, this time by sending him to the Queen with a letter instructing her to have him killed. On his way, the boy becomes lost in the forest (symbolic of adolescence) and takes refuge in a cottage inhabited by an old woman and a pack of thieves. They, however, take pity on him and change the letter while he is asleep, and he journeys on to marry the King's daughter.

Having lost his birth mother and then his foster parents, the youth is challenged once again by the King—this time to go to hell and fetch three golden hairs from the head of the Devil. On the way, he encounters three riddles. The watchman at one town asks him, Why did the market fountain, which once flowed with wine, become dry and no longer give even water? And, at another town, the gatekeeper asks, Why does a tree in the town that once bore golden apples now not even put forth leaves? Then a ferryman asks, Why must I always be rowing backward and forward and never be set free? The story continues:

When he had crossed the water he found the entrance to Hell. It was black and sooty within, and the Devil was not at home, but his grandmother was sitting in a large arm-chair.... "What do you want?" said she to him.... "I should like to have three golden hairs from the Devil's head," answered he.... "That is a good deal to ask for," said she; ... "but as I pity you , I will see if I cannot help you."

She changed him into an ant and said: "Creep into the folds of my dress, you will be safe there." ...

As the evening came on, the Devil returned home. No sooner had he entered than he noticed that the air was not pure. "I smell man's flesh," said he; "all is not right here." Then he pried into every corner, and searched, but could not find anything. His grandmother scolded him. "It has just been swept," said she, "and everything put in order, and now you are upsetting it again; you have always got man's flesh in your nose. Sit down and eat your supper."

When he had eaten and drunk he was tired, and laid his head in his grandmother's lap, and told her she should louse him a little. It was not long before he was fast asleep, snoring and breathing heavily. Then the old woman took hold of a golden hair, pulled it out, and laid it down beside her. "Oh!" cried the Devil, "what are you doing?" "I have had a bad dream," answered the grandmother, "so I seized hold of your hair." "What did you dream then?" said the Devil. "I dreamt that a fountain in a marketplace from which wine once flowed was dried up, and not even water would flow out of it; what is the cause of it?" "Oh, ho! if they did but know it," answered the Devil; "there is a toad sitting under a stone in the well; if they killed it, the wine would flow again."

The grandmother loused him again until he went to sleep and snored so that the windows shook. Then she pulled the second hair out. "Ha! what are you doing?" cried the Devil angrily. "Do not take it ill," said she, "I did it in a dream." "What have you dreamt this time?" asked he. "I dreamt that in a certain kingdom there stood an apple-tree which had once borne golden apples, but now would not even bear leaves. What, think you, was the reason?" "Oh! if they did but know," answered the Devil. "A mouse is gnawing at the root; if they killed it they would have golden apples again, but if it gnaws much longer the tree will wither altogether. But I have had enough of your dreams. If you disturb me in my sleep again you will get a box on the ear."

The grandmother spoke gently to him and picked his lice once more until he fell asleep and snored. Then she took hold of the third golden hair and pulled it out. The Devil jumped up, roared out, and would have treated her ill if she had not quieted him again and said: *"Who can help bad dreams?" "What was the dream, then?"* asked he, and was quite curious. *"I dreamt of a ferryman who complained that he must always ferry from one side to the other, and was never released. What is the cause of it?" "Ah! The fool,"* answered the Devil; *"when anyone comes and wants to go across he must put the oar in his hand, and the other man will have to ferry and he will be free."* As the grandmother had plucked out the three golden hairs, and the three questions were answered, she let the old Devil alone, and he slept until daybreak.

After leaving the grandmother, the youth delivers the needed messages to the ferryman (after first being rowed across the river), to the town with the unfruitful tree, and to the town with the dry well. In gratitude, the townspeople give him asses laden with gold. Upon his return home, the youth delivers the three golden hairs. The King is not quite content but wants to know how he found the asses laden with gold.

"I was rowed across a river," answered he, *"and got it there; it lies on the shore instead of sand." "Can I too fetch some of it?"* said the King.... *"As much as you like,"* answered he.... *The greedy King set out in all haste and when he came to the river he beckoned the ferryman.... When they got to the other shore he put the oar in his hand and sprang out.... From this time forth the King had to ferry, as a punishment for his sins. Perhaps he is ferrying still? If he is, it is because no one has taken the oar from him."*[3]

The foundling and the King stand as two alternatives to authority and leadership. The King represents the human ego that has embraced only outer kingship but also has become so enamored of the "kingdom" that any and every means is used to preserve that authority, as often can be seen in some schools.

Willfully, and with total disregard for human conscience, the King tries to kill the foundling by throwing his box in the sea, through the letter sent to the queen, and in sending the boy to hell. The authority and leadership invested in every human ego can be misused, thus making evil possible.

In contrast, the foundling, born with a caul, is "marked" for future greatness, as indeed is every child born into this world. He is carried on the life stream of water to the shore of his destiny, sleeps unscathed in a den of thieves, and returns from hell with the answers to his questions. He is not simply lucky (so many people today dismiss good fortune as luck). Rather, he is truly human; his thinking, feeling, and willing—in fact, all aspects of his being—are integrated. His heart forces are particularly strong, and he responds to each situation out of his humanity: He agrees to carry the letter, listens with openness to the three questions, places himself in the care of the old woman and later the grandmother, and delivers the messages at the end. By today's standards, he would be considered naive. But I maintain that the emerging ego, when working harmoniously with all aspects of human nature, is wise rather than clever. "Head" knowledge, being smart, would not have seen him through his journey. And herein lies the first gem from the fairy tale: Reasoning does not renew; working out of true humanity renews.

As parents, teachers, administrators, and advocates for educational improvement, how can we achieve this new humanity? The story gives us many clues. The foundling is raised for fourteen years by the miller and his wife. The life work of the miller is to work through the substance of nature (the grain) and prepare it for human consumption. The mill of life transforms both the pleasure and sorrow given by the world and creates new substance for life—consciousness that integrates. For it is not the bread alone that nourishes us; it is the love, the tending that goes into the baking. The miller and his wife took the foundling and raised him, only to let him go at age fourteen. Is this not the archetypal gesture of the teacher?

Often in the press of daily life, we cope with the sense impressions and outer circumstances surrounding us but do not have either time or inner resources to do the work of the miller and his wife, which is to work through the experiences, the pleasures and sorrows given us. These experiences that are not transformed become rocks in our system, eventually leading to stress and possibly burnout. The grinding of wheat, the processing of life's experiences, must happen if new substance is to be created. Along the way, we meet particular aspects of human nature that can challenge, awaken, and provide momentum for transformation: The toad under the well blocks the flow of wine, which could nourish as well as stimulate. The mouse, agile and nervous, can eat away at the tree, preventing growth that is the fruit of self-knowledge. And the ant, industrious and consumed by labor, can keep us earthbound unless we can step away and carry the three golden hairs home.

This brings us to the gold, not only in the three hairs from the head of the Devil but also in the asses laden with gold that expresses the gratitude of the townsfolk for solving their riddles. We know the expression "heart of gold." Gratitude expressed in gold is natural in that it is symbolic of the sun, the life-giving warmth of true wisdom. But why were the three "golden" hairs to be found on the head of the Devil?

The reader may want to ponder this quietly, for pondering often is more helpful than reading. In my musings, I have found that adversity, that which is ugly, evil, even painful, often yields remarkable insight, even if flashes of insight are but strands. Insight comes partly as a gift (from the grandmother) and partly through the courage to change (the ant) and pass through an experience. Each golden hair brought with it an insight, a solution to one of the riddles. This insight helped those in need— the towns and the ferryman—but not those unworthy, that is, the King. It is a curious culmination that the foundling for the first time gives the King a dose of his own medicine and sends him to the "other shore," knowing he will have to encounter the ferryman. Rather than simply being a punishment, this ending gives the King a chance to change and transform his one-sidedness. Renewal is about overcoming one-sidedness through encounter with others and the self. The true marriage of the foundling and the King's daughter is possible at the end, when wholeness is achieved.

Finally, we need to learn to protect ourselves from unwanted, unneeded influences. The "head under water" phenomenon is prevalent. This not only leads to stress but also prevents consciousness from going beyond the sense perceptions. In order to be "carried" by the water of life, as the foundling traveled in his box, we need to practice being sustained by the current and working with all that comes in the flow. This requires fluidity of our inner life and greater intimacy with the wisdom of the soul.

The Martyr

In "The Devil with the Three Golden Hairs," the boy helps others out of a genuine heartfelt humanity. There is a shadow side to caregiving as well, described by Carol Pearson:

> Martyrs not only feel deprived most of the time because they are sacrificing parts of themselves in the effort to get validation from God or from other people, but ... they often are also angry. It is essential to them that other people follow the same rules they have bought into because they cannot fully believe their sacrifices will work for them unless the same system works for other people....
>
> The reason martyrdom is such a trap for women is that it gets them off the hook on the issue of personal growth and of making a significant contribution to the world. When they fear they are not good enough or that they will be punished by the culture for having the audacity to declare themselves heroes with journeys to take, women can take refuge in the apparent virtue of self-sacrifice.[14]

Especially in the nurturing professions, such as nursing and teaching, caregivers, whether male or female, can easily fall into the trap of martyrdom through self-sacrifice. Motivated by genuine ideals and often sustained through love of the work, caregivers can "cross the line," a tenuous, often invisible line between healthy giving and becoming a martyr to the cause. When that line is crossed, it is hard to pull back again, since self-sacrifice becomes a kind of "refuge" from the rest of life's challenging realities.

In the process, the caregiver begins to lose a sense of self; rather than working from a place of self-identity and personal integration, the martyr looks to find meaning from the outside or the periphery of life. Those people and tasks that surround us can become the main focus of attention, and eventually the inner self is defined by those around us. We become what others want us to be. Identity is not grounded in the core of individuality but instead becomes dependent on the perpetual fulfillment of the needs of others. The more we give, however, the more those around us tend to need. Like Sarah in her desire to help her school, when the caregiver futilely tries to correct this dynamic and pull back a bit, feelings of guilt and anxiety set in, which, in turn, propel one back into self-sacrifice. One's sense of self-worth declines with each failed attempt, and eventually one almost becomes the "periphery"—the nurse and hospital, teacher and school, become one.

Instead of becoming the periphery, each person has the task today to fashion the inner life so that it is able to serve one's life aims truly. The shaping of the soul, a recurrent theme in this book, can be enhanced through the dynamic of sacrifice, as opposed to martyrdom. The "hero" is drawn, says Jung, with a fatal compulsion toward sacrifice and suffering. As described by Erich Neumann in *The Origins and History of Consciousness*, sacrifice helps a person step out of conformity, victimization, and the old order so as to learn to be an individual:

Whether his deeds are looked upon as services, as with Herakles, whose life, the life of many if not all heroes, is a series of strenuous labors and difficult tasks, or whether this symbolism takes the form of a bull-sacrifice as with Mithras, or crucifixion as with Jesus, or being chained to the Caucasus as with Prometheus, always and everywhere we meet with the motif of sacrifice and suffering.

The sacrifice to be made may mean giving up the old matriarchal world of childhood or the real world of the adult; sometimes the future has to be sacrificed for the sake of the present, sometimes the present so that the hero may fulfill the future. The nature of the hero is as manifold as the agonizing situations of real life. But always he is compelled to sacrifice normal living in whatever form it may touch him, whether it be mother, father, child, homeland, sweetheart, brother, or friend.

Jung puts it that the danger to which the hero is exposed is "isolation in himself." The suffering entailed by the very fact of being an ego and an individual is implicit in the hero's situation of having to distinguish himself psychologically from his fellows. He sees things they do not see, does not fall for the things they fall for—but that means that he is a different type of human being and therefore necessarily alone. The loneliness of Prometheus on the rock or of Christ on the cross is the sacrifice they have to endure for having brought fire and redemption to mankind.[15]

Suffering and sacrifice thus can become creative deeds when conventionality is overcome and new capacities are developed. We all are ruled by convention more than we realize. Society works in numerous and subtle ways to make us conform. The hero is a "free individual" who acts out of inner motivation with personal integrity and who has recognized the competing nature of outer constraints and through this understanding has achieved harmony and balance. The samurai and the knights of the Round Table are examples of this kind of hero who lives by a code that deals with both the inner spiritual life and outer behavior. When we act like heroes, we can enter into sacrifice or suffering and go through the experience to emerge with new strength and insight. This new strength gives us the courage to counter conformity and social norms when needed. Without this courage, we are continually at the mercy of people's opinions and the wish to please, to be recognized, and to be accepted. This is a hollow and empty space, whereas the hero's journey helps create richness that is self-sustaining.

The issue of sacrifice or even martyrdom for the teacher or parent then becomes one of timeliness and measure:

> Although rewards may not translate into material wealth or power in the world, genuine sacrifice is transformative and not maiming. How can you tell whether you are giving appropriately? When you are, doing so feels compatible with your identity, an outgrowth of who you are…. For many of us, making decisions about when and how much to sacrifice helps us learn who we are.[16]

Parents and teachers make daily choices, and these decisions, often made in the moment, help form the inner being that can negotiate that invisible line referred to earlier. That boundary has to be reconquered and redefined daily; otherwise one can lurch across it without realizing it. To lurch across or fall into situations creates imbalance, while working consciously can help a person return to that special center, or self, that acts like a compass in daily living. For, in fact, the duality of the angel, shadow, and other spiritual forces are continually at work in us. The question for the modern human being is this: How do I stand in relationship to what is working through me? And, yes, much works through us, just as light passes through the windows at Chartres. From a material perspective, we are ever so dense at times, but spiritually we are transparent.

It is also helpful to consider the whole matter from the perspective of the "other," that is, the person or people you are trying to help. We know that cooperative work is what makes the world a better place, but when does helping another become enabling? When are we simply supporting someone else's dependency or irresponsibility?

> Sometimes we persist in giving people who use our gifts and energy only to help themselves continue in a destructive pattern. This behavior is demonstrated most clearly by an enabler-addict symbiotic relationship in which one person seems totally selfless, helping the other, but actually is making it possible for the other to persist in a deadly habit such as a chemical addiction or other self-destructive actions…. An easy litmus test can determine whether one is giving or enabling. If when we give, we feel either used or smugly superior, it is time to look at what really is going on. Healthy giving is respectful of both the giver and the receiver. If Martyrs do not acknowledge that other able-bodied adults are capable of taking care of themselves, they are crippling them…. If Martyrs think giving is more virtuous than receiving, they are likely to give inappropriately and also to block the gifts they do receive, so they always feel shortchanged.[17]

Without belaboring the point, I suggest that caregivers look at the issue of self-sacrifice, which can potentially cast one in the role of martyr. Look at the patterns of interaction and the ways in which you respond to requests from others. Without becoming selfish, consider how to redress the balance of giving and receiving. If you are not able to take up a task, it might become a gift for someone else to do it, in that your stepping aside might provide an opportunity that attracts fresh talent and resources to the school.

Personal Change

> Change is disturbing when it is done *to* us, exhilarating when it is done *by* us.
>
> —Rosabeth Moss Kanter

Sarah, our teacher in the second chapter, had change forced upon her. Most of us would prefer to be an example of the second half of Kanter's statement. We have seen the hero's journey in the story of "The Devil with the Three Golden Hairs," and we have examined the shadow side of caregiving. Now that we are ready to begin our own journeys through the process of change, how can we go about it?

Many people are living cyclones. Their inner lives are in a state of suspended animation, while their outer lives are a constant whirl of activity. This incessant movement is not just an outer phenomenon; it manifests in the inner life as well. People today tend to hop from one thought to another, responding to stimuli but not initiating much out of inner volition. This hastiness creates more inner restlessness, and a vague feeling of dissatisfaction seeps in. As for active inner work, which could counteract this nervous energy, many say they don't have the time. Even those who know the value of meditation often feel that the events of the day crowd out the space for personal work. Another layer of guilt thus is added to the psychological baggage we carry around.

Although this comment may be too pointed for some, I feel that the final blow to personal renewal and change occurs when we give lip service to spiritual teachings without genuine practice. It is a subtle form of hypocrisy to sit in a meeting in which a meditative verse is read and then proceed to rumble around in discussion that clearly shows the lack of spirit working in the individuals present. It would perhaps be better not to have the pretense of spiritual striving than continually to invoke the language without the action.

This need not be the case. Countless spiritual teachings and indications from a variety of teachers can help people activate that inner core from which all life springs. For the purposes of this text, I will draw upon exercises given by Steiner for bringing about personal change. Whether or not one follows the philosophy of Steiner, I have found many resources in his work that can be applied in practical ways to everyday life situations. The intention of Steiner's philosophical work (anthroposophy) is to connect the spiritual in the human being with the cosmos, to connect us with the world in a meaningful way.

Today we often are compelled to take in information that does not speak to us, for example, through billboards along the road, commercials on TV, sales calls during dinner, and the like. This informational glut can damage the inner life, specifically, our ability to remember things. The balance to this challenge is to foster an active interest in what we do. While waiting in line at the motor vehicle bureau, find out about the person next to you in line. It is amazing how quickly the time passes in the midst of real conversation. Whether in conversation, reading, listening, or watching, the important thing is to take an active interest. This attitude quickens the inner life.

Creating connections is another example of enhancing the inner life. Whether trying to remember something or digesting a new thought, find ways to place the object of attention in context. One can compare and contrast, visualize the surrounding, and reflect on related experiences. For instance, if one has engaged in a particularly difficult phone call, rather than just dealing with it later—which pushes the response into the physical body, often to have it resurface during sleep—it is helpful to draw connections. How does this phone call compare with the last one like it? Are the circumstances different? How did I feel this time? Did we truly meet or just air our views? The more one is able to engage inwardly when a particular event occurs, the more the soul is given food for self-development.

A more direct approach is to effect a small change, to divert a habit and raise an action into new consciousness. Steiner gives many examples of this: changing one's handwriting, traveling a different path to work, or altering a routine habit in speech. To be attentive in a new way to what we are doing brings our innermost kernel of being into a more intimate connection with the task. We involve the inner being in the task, which refreshes and renews the life force described throughout this book. Another exercise that I have found particularly helpful is to remember backward. Look at the day as if moving backward through the events. This is especially helpful before sleep. It has the effect of release. (See more on this subject in the section on sleep.)

Steiner also suggests an exercise in which one carefully considers two or more aspects of a situation before making a decision. There is a pro and a con to everything, yet our vanity or self-absorption often prevents us from really seeing both aspects. It is especially helpful for decision-making to cultivate the practice of seeing both sides of an issue before deciding and implementing a choice. This is helpful on several levels: It helps one anticipate what will come as a response from those around one, and it gives one the inner experience to respond out of a kind of objectivity, rather than seeing criticism just as a personal attack. So much today is taken personally, which leads to much human anguish. The way to objectivity, in my view, is not to sanitize or reduce everything to hard "data" but rather to take the inner journey beforehand, thus preparing the inner self for what comes from outside. When the life of the soul is able to meet what comes from without on common ground, true objectivity is possible.

All this work on personal change calls for taking hold of one's conscious life and giving the soul new direction. In anthroposophical language, this means having the I, or higher self, grasp the emotional sensate life rather than letting consciousness flit about randomly. Instead of moving from one desire or wish to another, it is possible to take hold of these impulses and provide leadership. Plants respond almost completely to the natural environment. Animals also are amazingly responsive to the emotional as well as the physical climate. Isn't our task as human beings to do more than simply respond to what feels comfortable, to take up a conscious inner life so that we can do what is good and true even if it does not feel comfortable in the moment? We rest on the past when we make decisions based upon comfort level. We take a step into the future when we harness the will to change ourselves. If nothing else, renewal in schools depends upon the courage of individuals, like the boy in the story of "The Devil with the Three Golden Hairs," to make the journey of the hero to renew themselves.

I Need to Be Loved

In his pamphlet *The Sources of Inspiration of Anthroposophy*, Sigismund von Gleich speaks in the following way about the human journey:

> On account of strongly contrary headwinds and hurricanes, the steering of a person's boat of life can today become so firmly stranded on a sand bank that one can hardly set it afloat again out of one's own strength. In such cases from now on—so we may suppose—the "miracle" might come about that the divine Lord of Karma, for the sake of a higher necessity, loosens the little boat from the sand bank. With a simultaneous change of heart and soul such a person is thus given the possibility of new freedom of movement.
>
> But if a readiness for reconciliation based on deep understanding is not developed among human beings, then the associates of such an unfortunate one might be those who do not understand the change of heart and the new course of life embarked on. Not trusting, they can then only hinder his transformation. Hardly anything works so disastrously among human beings as the fatal tendency to nail someone down to earlier ways of action or traits of character which have perhaps recently, or even long since, been overcome. This lovelessness, a

rigidity out of self-complacency or love of ease, this it is whereby people continuously nail down—and crucify—one another.[18]

Fixed perceptions of one another can be overcome, given the will to do so. Not only must we ourselves meet the challenges of personal change but we also must set up an atmosphere for change for others and for ourselves. There are many exercises that can help. For those who wish to explore further, Steiner's book *How to Know Higher Worlds* contains many useful exercises. One that I have found helpful is to ask myself at the beginning of the day: "Can I discover something new about this colleague or parent today?" If one is so oriented, it is amazing how much there is still to discover, even regarding people with whom one has worked for years. It is especially helpful that this attitude actually supports the movement and positive development desired by the colleague in question; that is, my interest promotes the very flexibility and change that might be needed.

This is not to imply that changes are easy. We all carry wounds of one sort or another. Often unwittingly, we open the wound of another. Those wounds may be deep down or near the surface. We cannot avoid the hurt that comes with human interaction, but we do have options in how to work with the human condition. In the midst of the commotion of everyday life in a school, there are real people who have very basic needs. People want to be recognized, heard, loved. And human beings today have a great need to feel safe. Safety is something most teachers, parents, and administrators work with in an explicit way when it comes to the children, buildings, and supervision. But issues of safety with adult interactions are not recognized so easily. This is a delicate subject. If I once have confided in someone and this confidence was later broken, I now carry that as a wound. Am I likely to open up again? What are the conditions for healing?

There are no easy answers to these questions. I would like to share a few suggestions:

• A small victory can have ripple effects throughout the school. If one conversation can be "whole," if one parent or teacher feels their needs met, it will give that person the "magic" that will spread in each subsequent interaction.

• Fundamentally, the goal of the adult community surrounding a school is to create a culture of trust.

• Trust is enhanced when

> People listen with open minds and hearts;
>
> Talk straight;
>
> Share information;
>
> Recognize that people want to do good work on things that matter; assume best intentions, and you will experience best practices.

• People need each other and can be held together by a common purpose.

• If you want a culture of trust, you need people to participate, and they will participate if you recognize that they must be involved in things that affect them.

• Feelings and thoughts matter as much as deeds. And it is never too late to change.

In addition to exercises such as the ones mentioned elsewhere in this book, a special verse can become a companion on the inner path, such as Rudolf Steiner's Faithfulness Meditation:

> Create for yourself a new, indomitable perception of faithfulness. What is usually called faithfulness passes so quickly. Let this be your faithfulness:
> You will experience moments ... fleeting moments ... with the other person. The human being will appear to you then as if filled, irradiated with the archetype of his spirit.

And then there may be ... indeed will be other moments, long periods of time, when human beings are darkened. But you will learn to say to yourself at such times: The Spirit makes me strong. I remember the archetype, I saw it once. No illusion, no deception shall rob me of it.

Always struggle for the image that you saw. This struggle is faithfulness. Striving thus for faithfulness, we shall be close to one another, as if endowed with the protective powers of angels.[19]

5

TOOLS FOR THE INNER JOURNEY

Remember When ...

Norse mythology describes a timeless tree, Yggdrasil, with three giant roots and branches that spread over the whole world, even through heaven. Under the first root was the well of Urd, which was guarded by the three Norns, or goddesses of destiny. It was there that the gods gathered in council. Also known as the "Guardian Tree," Yggdrasil both nourished and suffered from the animals that lived there. Nidhogg the dragon gnawed at its roots; goats and deer jumped about in the branches, eating the tender shoots; and the squirrel Ratatosk ran up and down the tree carrying insults from Nidhogg to the eagle that lived at the top. The cooked fruit of Yggdrasil was said to ensure safe childbirth, and the dew from the tree was so sweet that the bees used it to make honey. Yet the tree was ever so old; parts were rotten, and parts were peeling. It whispered and groaned.

This mighty tree was nourished by the three Norns: Urd (Fate), Skuld (Being), and Verdandi (Necessity). They were thought to weave the destinies not only of humans but also of gods, dwarfs, and every living thing. Together they shared one eye. With it, they could see and understand the riddles of life, the working of humans and gods. They could see into the past, present, and future.

These images speak to the theme of renewal in a variety of ways. The tree represents life, fed by the well at its roots. Cultures around the world have recognized that water enhances life. In Asia, Indians view the Ganges as the life force of their land. Used not only for cleansing, water sustains life, as in the Grimm's tale "The Water of Life," described in *School as a Journey*. There is no birth without water. The doorway to the earth is through water; physical substance often is formed out of a watery existence. The well of the Norns comes from the hidden depths, giving life from unknown sources. But for me at least, the three Norns are the greatest riddle. With one eye, their vision, their wisdom, is extraordinary. What is it to be at the source of life, at the foot of the well? What is it like to be able to remember all that has happened? How does memory serve or detract from renewal?

For the sake of renewal, I want to stress that if one can practice detailed observation and active recollection, then inner relationships are created that are beneficial to the life force. Astute observation can give rise to vivid memory pictures that can lead, in turn, to healthy recollection, a process that supports life forces. Conversely, merely living with fleeting sense impressions that come and go like images on a screen leads to indistinct impressions and fumbling remembering, which saps the life forces. A good example of the latter is TV watching. When I was conducting a survey some years ago, I was astonished to discover how much time some teachers spent watching TV, even while advocating that children watch less. The fleeting images of television impair the ability to recollect. Life forces wither and along with them the ability to do simple things that require memory—Where did I put my cell phone? I just had it. It is so small. Did someone steal it? When little acts of remembering become challenging, chances are that one is suffering increased stress, diminished vitality, and more of a need for renewal.

Thus, remembering is not just about retrieval. It is a human process that can bring vitality to the soul, which, in turn, can result in knowledge that is experienced—that is, wisdom. Entering life situations with new wisdom and insight brings refreshment to other human beings. The practical side of this spiritual work is obvious. For teachers and their students, memory is vital to the learning process.

Today we live in a culture of the Now. Through the media and the many lures of materialism, an individual is enjoined to live for the moment, experience life, and "give yourself a treat today." Yet, ironically, when one really observes people, one can make the startling discovery that in terms of an inner life, few are really happy in the present. For many, the future looms full of expectation and carries with it considerable fear and trepidation. Many people are influenced by what may or may not happen in the future. It may be paying for a child's college education, saving for retirement, or the possibility of illness and suffering. Likewise the past runs like an underground stream through our lives. Experiences of family and friends, joy and suffering, success and failure live on in us more than usually is realized. I am convinced that learning to remember in a sound way can do tremendous good for human relationships today.

Some think of memory as a flash card system or a series of slides that can be retrieved at will. Others are stressed by so-called memory loss, even leading to the humorous story of the man who mistook his wife for a hat! What is memory, and how does it affect our vitality? One might begin by noticing two kinds of memory, one that is a retention of sequential and relational experiences, the other a flashing forth of a mental image. For instance, recall speaking with an elderly person who might have difficulty remembering what was served for lunch yesterday but can recollect in vivid detail an event or picture from childhood seventy years ago! Memory for such a person seems to live in the inner life as a reality, just waiting to be called up again. Even when there is short-term memory loss, a person may be able to bring forth remarkable experiences from the past. Thus recollection is an activity of the soul; it is a reconstruction, a creative act in which the invisible is made visible again.

Where do memory pictures reside when they are not being remembered? Many artists have used the theme of memory as a way to understand it. Memory is subtle, elusive, and intense. One only has to think of Marcel Proust and his madeleines, Colette's stories of her mother's garden, Lillian Hellman's remembrance of her friend Julia, and, on the screen, Federico Fellini's dreamlike images of his childhood. The Greeks personified memory and believed her to be the mother of the nine Muses. For an artist, then, memory is essential to the work of creation. Steiner believed that memory is held in the wellspring of life force. A trace remembrance, like a living melody, lives in the folds of this life force, retained as a concept. What we have been aware of rests in this "body" of formative forces, waiting to be awakened again by consciousness. The "body" of our feelings and emotions, the seat of consciousness, is the awakener. In other words, if I suddenly smell bread baking, it awakens the conscious memory of a time when I sat in my great-aunt's kitchen as a child and watched her pull fresh bread from a wood stove.

What sets the awakening process in motion? The inner organ through which the object of memory is again recognized and activated is the human ego. It shakes itself awake during the act of recollection. That which was below the threshold of consciousness hovers, phantomlike, asleep, and then is reawakened as a memory. Just as the life forces continually form and recreate the physical body outwardly, so inwardly the life forces form and hold the memories given by life. It is interesting to watch someone trying to remember: the finger may tap impatiently, the person may walk up and down or fiddle with a pencil. But when contact is made and the memory is found, the body usually is completely still.

Thus, remembering is an affair involving the whole human being. The impetus for recollection comes from the ego. The senses connect with consciousness, which grasps and seeks the memory; the life force retains it; and the physical body rests quietly in order for the process to take place. Understandably, when the physical body is ill, it is harder to remember.

That part of the human being that I have been calling the ego is like the driver of a vehicle, the Greek charioteer holding the reins of a horse. This ego, unique to each human being, identifies strongly with past experiences and in so doing identifies itself continually with itself. In remembering, a person likewise is experiencing, judging, and refashioning self-identity. This grasping of memory becomes the feeling of being within oneself. This is the spiritual ground of intuition. For those who want practical exercises to improve these processes, I suggest the following:

• Since memory, as I have described it, is a matter of the whole body, use the body. Rhythm helps us take things into the organism. Like an actor learning lines, walk or move rhythmically when memorizing. You can even adapt the words you are learning to a rhythmic pattern.

• If you are trying to recall a poem or a passage from a book and cannot remember a word, put an arbitrary one in the blank space. Later, see if you can replace the arbitrary word with the word needed.

• Use the picture quality of memory to remember a person, event, or place. Draw the picture inwardly, supplying as much detail as possible. The person may just pop into your mind during the process!

• Practice, at the same time of day, remembering to do something that is not essential, for example, switching a book on the shelf. This exercise, if done regularly, can strengthen the will to remember.

• Finally, since the life force is crucial to good memory, do the things that are best for engendering life forces. Eat well, exercise, cultivate a hobby, and enjoy the arts. If we are in tune, the inner life can better harmonize the needs of past, present, and future.

Reading Destiny

Whereas the Norse Gods went to Yggdrasil and consulted the three Norns of Fate, Being, and Necessity, the parent and teacher today need to learn to read destiny for themselves. When training for lifeguard certification in high school, I was reminded again and again that when one is caught in the swift current of a river while undertaking a rescue, it is best to swim diagonally with the current. Anyone who has experienced the flow of a river knows to respect the power of that moving water. So it is with destiny. Yes, the swimmer is important too, but it helps tremendously if one is able to respect the fundamental current, or destiny, working in this lifetime.

It really astonishes me to see teachers and parents occasionally expend inordinate energy and time fighting the current. This arises when a parent does not truly support or feel comfortable with a teacher or a school, yet avoids addressing the issues of concern directly. The parent can feel "out of it" and at the same time trapped in an untenable situation. Or a teacher might continue teaching while feeling the tug of another career. These counter-current positions in life contribute to a general sense of unease in a school community. As mentioned in other contexts, a school tends to absorb, like a sponge, all that lives in its surroundings. One way to strengthen our schools is to develop the capacity to read destiny, our own and that of those we care about. For example, if it is clear that a program that has been approached in the same way every year is now outdated or that there is not the time, the people, or the energy to effect it, this is the current of destiny. It should be seen as a need for change. As a Waldorf teacher, I have found Steiner's works full of practical suggestions. I have adapted a few in the steps outlined here. These steps do not result in instantaneous insight, as if the three Norns have answered all our questions. Instead, we must take responsibility and do the work ourselves. In my experience, working with destiny allows for moments when one is able to see the larger reality and then ask the right question at the right time or make a simple change that brings realignment with the current of life.

> Only when you are most low
> can you receive the highest,
> only when you are most empty
> can you be filled,
> only when you are truly at rest
> can I be active in you.[20]

Here are some ways in which one can see where the future is leading:

• If you are prevented from doing one thing, be very attentive to what comes into the alternative space. (For example, if you miss a bus you had planned to catch, look out for what happens while you are waiting for the next one!) We are usually too preoccupied with disruptions to our conscious plans, desires, and so forth to sense potential meaning/intention from our unconscious.

• Carry images of your life situation into sleep. Do not judge, interpret, or analyze. Simply offer them to your unconscious with a question: "What shall I do? What is this about?" The following day, look and listen to messages from the outer world. Maybe you will overhear a remark, not even addressed to you, or notice a road sign or some other outer phenomenon that speaks something meaningful to you. Repeat this process for three nights and days. Trust your perceptions, even if you don't immediately make sense of them. You are beginning to activate, or become more conscious of, a "force field" between the inner and outer, which carries your destiny more truly than does the everyday ego consciousness.

• Any significant event you would like to understand more fully also can be carried into sleep for three nights. Evoke the experience strongly, pictorially, before sleep. Note any changes in your perception or feelings on subsequent days. Frequently, by the fourth morning you will find that you have a new attitude and a new sense for action.

• Recognize that every choice takes you down one path and leaves others untrodden. And while you are standing on one piece of ground, no one else can occupy it! We sometimes cling to places, believing that if we move, the world will collapse or stop turning! We may be depriving another person of their next step.

• Question what steps we might offer another through opportunities we can bring to him or her.

Learning to Pray Again

The scene is a subway train in New York City. The time is 7:30 a.m. The lights flicker on and off as the train gathers speed, revealing rows of people, heads buried in newspapers or silently staring straight ahead into space. The noise and early hour prevent conversation, and the bodies remain arranged side by side, with no more than an occasional bump of human interaction. The train grinds to a halt. There is a frenzy of activity as people rush out and others rush in, only to repeat the numbing ride from here to nowhere. The steel, noise, artificial light, and human isolation in the subway of life has placed many in a trap: predictable stations in which to get on and off, little human warmth, and time that is measured by endurance. Those trapped in the subway car of materialism suffer silently inside. There is the appearance of motion but without much purpose.

It is amazing how the modern experience of living seems to conspire to keep us running, dealing with the here and now, avoiding the underlying issues and realities of our lives. We saw an example of this in Sarah's story. We spend more and more time absorbing information without a chance to process it, gaining knowledge about things without finding the composure to develop wisdom. With technology we have become more productive, but are we really happier? By giving themselves over to external impressions, many feel they have become estranged from themselves. We spread ourselves thin in every direction, and our life forces are expended with abandon. At the end of another hectic day, exhaustion sets in, mind-numbing, complete exhaustion that makes the body feel like a vegetable. Watching TV can transfer this lethargy to our inner life as well. A few hours go by with little to show for the time spent. Listless, we fall asleep, only to wake all too soon and begin the routine again.

By letting the outer world rule us, we have created a barrier to the very composure and healthy inner life that could renew and replenish. The preoccupation with external demands has stopped higher, stronger divine forces from unfolding in us. Like Sarah, sometimes it takes a crisis to shake things up enough to refocus. It shows us that we have the freedom to choose where we pay attention, to decide how we lend ourselves to each day. There are moments when we can find the way to extend beyond immediate preoccupations, to go further than the momentary concerns of the ego. Urged on by a crisis, the inner kernel of self can initiate new development of the ego.

This self-initiated striving, even if it is just to understand something more fully, can create a wonderful feeling of inner warmth. By inwardly engaging, rather than numbing out, the inner self is able to re-create. This happens in artistic practice, meditation, and prayer. The warmth generated by such self-directed activity can make a soul that was losing itself in externalities collect itself again through the inner life.

One thing that helps tremendously is to shed the "control and mastery" attitude of the materialistic rat race of life. If one can find a few moments to take up an imponderable, one realizes how little we truly control out of self-will. Teachers in Zen Buddhism use koans, short vignettes or questions as imponderables for meditation purposes. The koan cannot be understood by logic but brings the student to direct intuitive realization of the Greater Reality. Isshu Miura and Ruth Fuller Sasaki, in *The Zen Koan*, quote these well-known examples: "A monk asked Master Joshu: 'Has the dog Buddha-nature or not?' Joshu answered: 'Moo!'" And "Hakuin Zenji used to say to his disciples: 'Listen to the sound of the Single Hand!'" Miura and Sasaki go on to explain that all living beings are Buddha or endowed with Buddha-nature. Furthermore, even though all sounds are correctly broadcast, our receiving instruments are lost in emission of our own noise, and we are unable to detect subtleties.[21]

Here are examples of imponderables from our own culture. After considering them, see if you can come up with your own koan or imponderable:

- When expecting a child, rather than finding the answer through technology to the question of whether it is a boy or a girl, hold the question.

- Upon the birth of a child and in the days, weeks, and years that follow, ask this question: Who is this child?

- Rather than doing yard work just for the sake of getting the job done, pause, as did Sarah after her illness, and ask: What is it like for that seed at the moment of sprouting?

- As when I made my decision to take on a first grade years ago, one might take an evening walk away from the streetlights and ask: Are the stars speaking to me this evening?

- In a meeting, one might wonder: How is it that the solution to a problem often surfaces in a way that is least expected?

- In reawakening the joy and wonder in a marriage, one might ask from time to time: Did we know each other before we met?

There are as many of these imponderables as there are stars in the night. Which one you choose matters less than the reality of living with a thought that defies ordinary logic. If one lives with an imponderable for a time, one can experience a feeling of submission, of devotion to that which is greater than I. We are led beyond ourselves. In the process, we engender feelings of light and warmth. The light is symbolic of freeing the soul of the need to have answers to all questions. It is freedom from concern for what comes to us out of the future and freedom from anticipation. The feeling of warmth is symbolic of the realization that through the past we have only glimpsed the divine, but we can now create new feelings and sensations that work with the life force within us.

A sense of spiritual submission prepares us to meet what comes out of the future. Teachers and parents live in a perpetual state of anticipation of the unexpected. Children by their very nature defy predictability! Instead of living in fear and anxiety, when we live with and cultivate the imponderables in the inner life, we find that we can gradually learn to meet everything that comes to us with new certainty, hope, and personally-generated confidence.

In everything, there is the wisdom of the world, held like morning dew in the petals of bright flowers. The seeker can find secrets that are waiting to be discovered in all of nature—the formation of rocks, plants, animals, humans, and even the stars. The creative forces that brought everything into existence are often hidden, even obscured from vision by the material substantiality of "things." The wisdom is found when we are able to see through the illusion of matter and find the wellspring of creative life, the movement, growth, and transformation rather than the finite, fixed objects of the world around us. One can begin by simply feeling the grandeur and immensity of it all. Devotion can lead to receptivity, which can generate insight and new confidence in the wisdom of the world. This wisdom shines before us. Our striving, especially in the arts, meditation, and prayer, makes it possible for this wisdom of the world to shine through our longing for the highest. Illumination arises from the reality of devoted inner striving.

Sleep

In the many books, articles, research projects, retreats, and conferences available to teachers, and in the government commissions and public debate about school renewal, I rarely hear any mention of the role of sleep. When asked to comment on this subject, most people respond, "Of course, if only I could get more sleep, it would help a lot. But with my schedule, I am just not able to get to bed on time." And most acknowledge that a good night's sleep makes a world of difference. One can be a completely different person, depending on the quality and quantity of sleep. Yet the topic has received little public attention with regard to our schools.

In this section, I would like to characterize aspects of sleep and how sleep relates to personal and organizational health. We live in a time of nervous overstimulation, a kind of perpetual wakefulness. As discussed earlier, in the third chapter, our lights, beepers, telephones, cars, and other modern conveniences tend to keep our nerves in a state of agitation. The pace of life is such that we seem to be rushing from one thing to another. It takes a tremendous effort of will to carve out an oasis of sanity, a period of uninterrupted quiet. It is almost as if the world today is conspiring to prevent the kind of peace and contemplation needed for spiritual life.

One would think that all this outer activity would at least guarantee a good night's sleep, but, unfortunately, more and more people suffer from insomnia and other sleep disorders. The day can wind up being so hectic that it is difficult to slow down enough simply to sleep. As a result, more and more people are running around during the day in a state of suspended exhaustion. Some of the consequences include these:

- Short tempers and general impatience with anything that takes more than a few minutes;
- Speech that is monosyllabic, tense, and abstract;

- Errors of judgment in matters large and small;

- More interpersonal misunderstanding and conflict;

- Decisions that are made out of personal imbalance that lead to organizational unease;

- Less care, love, and devotion to children and others who matter in our lives.

In fact, if one wish could be granted to me on behalf of school renewal, I would ask for significant improvement in the quality of sleep afforded to parents and teachers. No other change has the potential to do more good than simply eliminating the state of chronic exhaustion found by the end of the week in most schools.

What happens during sleep? Many people view sleep as a sort of "timeout" from life, a necessary function of human existence. But the more I read of contemporary studies on sleep and the indications given at the turn of the century by Steiner, the more I have come to realize that sleep is a highly functioning state of consciousness. My first indication of this potency came during the process of collating the results of a survey I had conducted on teacher renewal. More than one hundred teachers in dozens of public and Waldorf schools were surveyed. One of the questions asked was this: When do you receive most of your inspirations for teaching, in the evening or the early morning? Because most teachers prepare in the evening, logic would have rendered an answer in favor of the evening. However, 66% of the public school teachers and 71% of the Waldorf teachers reported receiving most of their inspirations for teaching in the early morning or, in other words, after sleep. My survey question led me to another question: What is it about sleep that allows for inspiration and the energy associated with inspired teaching?

Great poets and writers have referred to sleep as vital and nourishing. Among them, Shakespeare had this to say: "Sleep that knits up the raveled sleave of care, / The death of each day's life, sore labor's bath,/ Balm of hurt minds, great nature's second course,/ Chief nourisher in life's feast."[22] And in Cervantes's *Don Quixote*, Sancho Panza says: "Blest be the man who first invented sleep—a cloak to cover all human imaginings, food to satisfy hunger, water to quench thirst, fire to warm cold air, cold to temper heat, and, lastly, a coin to buy whatever we need."[23]

From my own study of Steiner's work and others, I have come view sleep as a form of consciousness that allows for a kind of processing not possible with daytime consciousness. Throughout the various stages of sleep, we "digest" the previous day and open ourselves to the influences of something greater than ourselves. Sleep can be seen as a mighty outbreath that balances the inbreath of the day, with all the sense impressions that we absorb. At the moment of falling asleep, there is a kind of loosening, or letting go. One can experience this if one is attentive: As the body rests in bed, the limbs gradually start to float; the head is the last part of the body to let go of consciousness. Just before sleep one can experience a kind of swimming, as if one is rocked by the gentle waves of a greater ocean of existence. In the morning, one tends to wake up in the limbs first, and only gradually does consciousness reenter the rest of the body. It is possible that on an early Monday morning, one might move about the house, getting coffee and breakfast, while still essentially asleep in the head. If one is a morning person, the process of arriving is more rapid; if one is an evening person, the spiraling movement of consciousness over a twenty-four-hour period is more gradual.

During the day, we occupy ourselves with sense impressions and our responses to what people say, do, and think. At night, the departure of our daytime consciousness allows for conversation with our inner beings. As we go through the various stages of sleep, Steiner suggests that we are refreshed by spiritual beings who take an interest in our progress. Steiner described these spiritual beings as angels, archangels, and *archai*. The angels are most connected to our work as single individuals; they are closest to us. The archangels work with groups of people, such as a school community or a nation. And the *archai* oversee the flow of time. The degree of involvement on these three levels depends upon how we have spent our daytime hours. If we have taken the time to work with nature, with the growing and blossoming world of the plant kingdom, the first stage of sleep is enhanced. If one has had real conversation, a human interaction of a significant kind in which the art of speech is practiced, another stage of sleep is enhanced. Finally, we bring a third realm of "gifts" to the world of sleep, namely, our movements during the day. Each step or hand gesture and our satisfaction or dissatisfaction with these movements means something in our encounters during sleep. It matters how we move through the day, what we say and how we relate to the environment. In short, the spiritual beings we meet during sleep can help us more intensely if we have lived our daytime hours in a healthy way.

All this can be experienced practically through self-observation. Keep a sleep journal and record how you have spent the day in terms of the considerations mentioned here. Then, upon waking, make note of the quality of your sleep. Did you wake up refreshed or groggy, ready for a new day or tired and dissatisfied? I have found that after a day in an airplane, for instance, my sleep back home is less refreshing. Conversely, if I am able to have a least one real conversation, take a walk in nature, or even care for a houseplant, my sleep is influenced for the better. How we spend our day matters in terms of sleep, and how we sleep influences how we meet our children and create community in schools.

Sleep also serves as a kind of review in which life events are processed. As I mentioned, sleep has to digest the day, and given the kinds of days some of us have, this can be a tall order at times! One helpful exercise is to review the day before falling asleep, thus beginning the process. This "viewing backwards" means finding a few minutes before sleep to look at the events of the day in reverse order, beginning with the evening and going backward to the early-morning experiences. As one becomes more adept at this, one not only can name the sequence backward but also can reverse the events themselves. One can try to picture oneself walking backward or cooking in reverse order. It is very difficult to do this, but after a while it is possible to take on a recall of the speech used in conversations. It is important, however, not to begin a new dialogue and create new material while trying this exercise. Just review what has occurred.

It is thus possible, by looking at life experiences, to place them in a more secure way in the tapestry of personal biography. Recently I received a phone call from someone I had not heard from in many years. It was wonderful to speak again after so much time. That evening in my review, it was possible to see how this friend had influenced me in ways that had continued long after our time of working together. Even when there is an unpleasant daytime experience, the review can help sort things out. Backward review can let things settle, create an inner acceptance, and lighten the burden for the processes of sleep.

This practice relates to another of my favorite exercises, one that can be of great help in our parent/teacher school communities:

> If we attain the calm inner survey, the essential is severed from the non-essential. Sorrow and joy, every thought, every resolve, appear different when we confront ourselves in this way. It is as though we had spent the whole day in a place where we beheld the smallest objects at the same close range as the largest, and in the evening climbed a neighboring hill and surveyed the whole scene at a glance.... The value of such inner tranquil self-contemplation depends far less on what is actually contemplated than on our finding within ourselves the power which such inner tranquillity develops.[24]

If we can live our days with an ever-greater sense for the essential and the nonessential and then do a thorough review of the day each evening, we have the possibility of working out of a calm inner center. Rather than rushing about putting out brush-fires and trying so hard to please and satisfy those around us, we can be ourselves. In being true to the Inner Self, we truly give and love more than before.

When I was a class teacher, I often asked myself in the evening how I could help a particular child in my class. I would try to picture the child in the classroom or at play and simply ask the question: What is she or he asking for? Many times I awoke in the morning with new insight or understanding of the child in question. It was not as if I suddenly knew everything I always wanted to know about the student, but there would be a next step, a way to begin working in a new way. Thus, in my experience, the morning inspirations came in bite-size portions, but when taken together, they helped me meet the inner striving of the children in my care.

I also have found sleep preparation helpful in terms of collegial relationships. When a relationship was strained, I tried to spend a few minutes before sleep picturing the person in his or her most ideal state—a moment when I experienced the very best that teacher had to offer. That image of the "higher self" then accompanied me into sleep, and often in the following days a new harmony or sense of clarity would enter the relationship. Often we find ourselves inadvertently strengthening polarities, such as reacting in a way that makes the other person even more a caricature of his true self. The trick is to step out of the ego-to-ego dynamic at times and instead adopt a path of inquiry: Who is he? With the maturation that can come during sleep, it is possible to tune into the striving of the other person on a more fundamental level. What is he or she trying to accomplish in this life? How am I perhaps serving as a foil for this development? What am I learning about myself in this interaction? What is my task with this person?

Even if we never come to any answers to these questions, the very asking opens up the situation so that spiritual insight has a greater chance of entering. Insight is like a beam of light; it is nonmaterial and flashes forth when least expected. Between the flashes, however, are long periods in which one has to go on asking the questions. One can only hope that at least we are asking the right questions, questions that plow up the soil of the soul, questions that keep us alive. And if we are inwardly alive, in touch with our own genius, we can be renewed through sleep. As Rudolf Steiner says in his verse "The Holiness of Sleep":

> I go to sleep.
> Till I awaken
> My soul will be in the spiritual world,
> And will there meet the higher Being
> Who guides me through this earthly life—
> Him who is ever in the spiritual world,
> Who hovers about my head.
> My soul will meet him,
> Even the guiding Genius of my life.
> And when I waken again
> This meeting will have been.
> I shall have felt the wafting of his wings.
> The wings of my Genius
> Will have touched my soul.[25]

6

RELATING TO ONE ANOTHER

Soul Landscapes

Just as one can take a walk in the mountains and experience the splendor of rock, tree, and ridge, so it is possible to orient oneself toward the inner landscape. As humans, awake in our sense organs of sight, touch, and hearing, we tend to experience the world of outer phenomena as primary, as the only reality. Many situations and problems are approached from the perspective of outer phenomena: What did he say? How many people were there? What is the cost? These questions are valid and necessary for meeting the world, but they are by nature limited in scope. Where human beings are concerned, one has to look also at the landscape of the inner life. What is living through her words? What is the nature of his experience, and how is it playing into his language? Who is it that is speaking? If one is able to work with both types of inquiry, the sense world can begin to serve as validation of inner experience, and the inner experience can help us find the path when the outer trail comes to a dead end. When a school or organization appears to be stuck and cannot expand, build, or start a new program, it is a condition that is rooted in the inner world and not just a matter of funding. If one frees the inner dynamic, as related here and elsewhere in this book, the outer logjam can be relieved. Both inner and outer explorations are needed for school renewal.

In Relation to Different Types of People

As spiritual companions, we are equal in our striving. But the inner life of each individual can be different. What is experienced inwardly influences the outer response. One person might focus on the words that were said and the commitment to a task that may or may not be there, while another person might experience the inner struggle, the anguish that played beneath the surface. One person might want to do something about the situation right away, and another might feel the need to listen more and engage in exploratory conversation. In her work with colleagues and parents, Sarah's responses were based on her intuition. She responded differently to some than to others from her intuitive feelings. But when she became stressed, and especially when the school was without her leadership for some months, this nuanced response was neglected. For example, when one mother came in to talk about the student expulsion, the administrator simply reiterated the school's decision and overlooked that she was asking to engage in a conversation, a dialogue. The mother went away more frustrated than before.

Fluidity of the inner life, mentioned earlier, is the capacity to move inwardly to meet a given situation. Regardless of gender, race, or culture, it is possible to be human, which is to meet what is presented in a respectful embrace of empathy. In many cases, it is the person doing the listening who has to exert the most fluidity. In my experience, it is an amazing reality that if only one person practices this mindful openness to the soul or inner landscape, the other person is lifted into a new place. The journey together begins with the soul. A person working on self-transformation can experience more than one reality of inner life and can travel inwardly as needed.

Living in the Presence of the Other

The young mother with a newborn child breathes, eats, sleeps, and even moves in relation to the all-pervading presence of the baby. Even if a mother is several rooms away, she knows how her little one is doing. It is not just a matter of hearing the cry or being in tune with the breathing; the mother knows in the depths of her being how it is with her child. She lives in the presence of the being she has brought into the world.

Another example from adult life comes from the experience of being in love. Whether this happens in youth, midlife, or old age, the experience is archetypal. To be in love is to live every moment aware of the other. Daily tasks continue, and one might even be separated geographically at times, yet the presence of the other is felt, a gentle wafting through all daily events. What one does has relevance in terms of the loved one; every decision and experience become relational. Even when one is not conscious of the other person, there is a flowing, moving, and breathing of life that is different because of the fullness of heart. Particularly in the transition moments of consciousness, waking and falling sleep, one can experience "living with" the other.

In terms of the social fabric of our schools, it is possible to cultivate one's inner life so that when needed, the same "presence," a certain attunement, can be achieved with a child, colleague, or parent. This can be done in a variety of ways, but a couple of suggestions here may be helpful:

- Attend. A first step can be simply observational, seeing and listening more acutely. Tuning in can be like giving birth to a baby, in that the other is given space in which to become. Let the person simply "be" at this stage. Do not try to intervene. In fact, injecting oneself into a situation can shut down the process and thwart what is intended in this exercise.

- Live with. This means walking the path together. Just think of the many hours a mother spends with her newborn! Living with the other requires that, at times, the thinking, analytical side of human nature become silent for a bit. Just experience, notice, and enjoy the mystery of the other person.

- Let go. We tend to fixate on a question, problem, or person and get so wrapped up in it that we can no longer move. This fixation is like a stranglehold; the air stops flowing. Instead, let go. Remove oneself from the situation, question, or challenge. This has a freeing effect.

- Finally, reengage with love. Turning oneself back to the person, one can find a new connection. That connection, which is not demanding but giving, tends to open the eyes of the inner landscape. The best vehicle for entry is the practice of love, not the "being in love" described earlier, but the exercise of love for the sake of the person you are meeting. Even a difficult person can be approached in this way. Not everyone is lovable, but everyone responds in the end to selfless love and compassion.

When one is able to exercise this new faculty, it is possible to read the inner landscape of self and others as one might read a book. The colors and contours of this landscape can be rich beyond expectation, especially if one has the character and inner standing to meet that which is revealed.

To Be Alone or Together

In *Return of the Prodigal Son*, Henri Nouwen describes an aspect of life that could have been addressed directly to Sarah and her colleagues at the Morning Glory Waldorf School:

> Caught in this tangle of needs and wants, I no longer know my own motivations. I feel victimized by my surroundings and distrustful of what others are doing or saying. Always on my guard, I lose my inner freedom and start dividing the world into those who are for me and those who are against me. I wonder if anyone really cares. I start looking for validations of my distrust. And wherever I go, I see them, and I say: "No one can be trusted." And then I wonder whether anyone ever really

loved me. The world around me becomes dark. My heart grows heavy. My body is filled with sorrows. My life loses meaning. I have become a lost soul.[26]

To choose to work on one's self and to find the balance between being with others and being alone is part of the exhilaration of personal change, as stated by Rosabeth Kanter in chapter 4 of this text. Many people today, however, are like the prodigal son, in that they have become disconnected from what gives life and nourishment—namely, family, friends, and community—through no conscious choice of their own. The condition of being alone is a particularly modern situation. Inheritance, family tradition, and community festivals and rituals give less to us in our world today. We have gained tremendous freedom, but it has come with the possibility of being alone as never before. What we have in common today must be consciously sought out, cultivated, and cherished.

Another way of looking at this dilemma is in terms of the isolation imposed by the day-to-day business of life and work, in which we can find ourselves trapped in an impersonal rat race of never-ending busy work. Warren Bennis describes it this way: "Routine work drives out nonroutine work and smothers to death all creative planning, all fundamental change."[27] The assembly line of life can put us in a relationship to daily events that limits creative expression, initiative, and community building. This isolation affects school renewal, because schools are founded precisely on the principle of community. Whether one goes back to John Dewey, Leo Tolstoy, or Friedrich Froebel, one finds that schools always have been concerned with experiencing learning in context with peers, so as to prepare for the social needs of our times. Schools often have been seen as laboratories of democracy. The social curriculum—learning how to get along together—is a major goal in most classrooms.

If one places the modern adult, who feels isolated and alone, in a setting called a "school," in which community building is essential, one faces an interesting juxtaposition. The very nature of a school calls upon that which can be most difficult for adults today. We frequently are thrown into social structures that seem to challenge us, confound us, and create untold frustration when things don't go smoothly. The question then becomes, How can the individual, autonomous and free, join in with others to create new community experiences surrounding our schools? There are many ways to approach this issue, and, in fact, most of the chapters of this book can be seen as a response to this question. But for this section I would like to take the point of view of two human qualities that strongly influence group life, namely, sympathy and antipathy.

Antipathy

This word may seem to have only negative connotations, but as an expression of inner life, I want to characterize antipathy in a way that can expand upon the themes raised in this chapter. Antipathy can be described as an inner quality that helps differentiate between "self" and the environment. Rather than bringing everything in, we use antipathy to hold things at arm's length to see more clearly. By separating ourselves from the environment in this way, our I, or individuality, is able to experience itself as distinct. Thus, through antipathy we are able to wake up to "self," collect and make sense of experiences, and relate them to personal, core issues. If it is carried to an extreme, antipathy can result in shutting off, pushing away, or withdrawing from others.

Sympathy

In contrast, sympathy can be described as an inner quality that helps us merge with others and the environment. In connecting sympathetically with what is around us, we lose self-consciousness in relation to others. We empathize, connect, and "live with" to the extent that we are able to enter into the experiences of the other and forget the self. Those with strong sympathetic forces frequently are seen as being socially adept. Spiritually, this ability to extend oneself into the other can become the capacity to connect with the divine.

Sympathy and antipathy are constantly at play within groups. There are times when generous listening and compassion can bring the forces of sympathy to the fore, and the group senses a merging of different strands, a consensus of the heart. But there are also times when the need to differentiate, examine, and explore options requires forces of antipathy, which are just as necessary. Sight can be clouded by sympathy and sharpened through healthy antipathy. When sympathy prevails too strongly, there is a tendency for a group to start smothering the individual identities of its members. The air becomes thick, and it seems hard to breathe because of all the warmth. Thinking can be suppressed, and it becomes increasingly difficult for anyone to raise a question or objection that might destroy the sympathetic soup of conformity. Likewise, when antipathy grows too strong in a group, a chill sets in. Suddenly everything is called into question, and the group becomes a collection of separate individuals. Clarifications are constantly needed; agreement is often conditional and transitory. The sense of the "whole" can be lost.

The trick, of course, is to allow an alternation between sympathy and antipathy, expansion and contraction. Once again, language can be a great help, in that the phrasing of questions or observations will influence the tone of the group in terms of how we view the climate. For instance, if one begins each contribution with "I agree with so and so," then the language culture can tip the scales toward sympathy. If, however, one uses phrases such as "actually, what I meant was" or "in fact, I think we should," then the forces of antipathy grow. A good facilitator will notice the spiritual climate of the group and the language used and will try to redirect and balance the conversation. All it takes is one person—the facilitator or someone else—to redress the balance.

Why is balance so important for group work? For one thing, if one form of expression or another is overly used, those who are inwardly living in the counter-gesture will be silenced. This is a crucial aspect of group work in schools. If a person is silenced repeatedly, there is a kind of subtle repression that over time can lead to antisocial behavior. When the emphasis on agreement is too strong, for instance, it is very hard for a parent or teacher with questions or suggestions to participate. Yet participation is a human necessity. Participation in a school community is as vital as breathing is to the human body. One can suspend breathing or participation only so long before the forces of death set in. It is the responsibility of every adult in a school community to fight for health, which in group life means participation.

I believe that we can do even more, for we can take responsibility for our own feelings rather than project them onto the group. Some time ago, I had a difficult morning. The phone rang just as I was headed out the door. Then I pulled into the gas station on the wrong side of the pump and realized it after I had turned off my engine and was fumbling for my credit card. The first e-mail I read was from someone asking a question that could have been answered easily elsewhere. Matters continued in this way. By the time I entered my department meeting I was out of sorts. I felt a great desire to dump my grumpiness on others. Fortunately, the meeting began with a variety of lighthearted items, and by the time I began to participate, I had shed my feelings of frustrations and was able to be there for the group. I doubt any of my colleagues was affected by my mood.

We are not always so lucky. Letting go of, or at least taking responsibility for, feelings is not always easy. And things become complicated when one enters the web of human interaction, because every thread we weave elicits reactions from others, to which we then feel compelled to respond. One tool I have found invaluable is to separate evaluation from observation. Here is an example of the difference: "The fifth-grade reports have not been mailed to the parents" (observation). "The fifth-grade teacher does not write his reports on time" (evaluation). These statements may both be true. The question is, Which mode of expression is most helpful? Generally, I have found that observing again and again, from different vantage points, helps construct a bridge between people and the realities of life, while evaluation needs full sanction ahead of time, that is, we must agree that this is an evaluative moment before taking that step. For those readers who are interested in pursuing the topic of language, I suggest *Nonviolent Communication: A Language of Compassion* by Marshall B. Rosenberg, published by PuddleDancer Press in 1999.

What amazes me is that so often the values we carry into the classroom are not transferred to adult interactions in and around our schools. A good teacher strives for the growth and participatory learning of all her students, but in collegial relations, we often see the opposite. Agreement becomes the goal; participation is a necessary inconvenience. "If only you would all agree with me, we could go home and get on with our preparation" is sometimes the unspoken message. Because most people want to oblige and not ruffle any feathers, many do shut down and quietly go along, only to internalize what should have been worked with in the group. Over time, this constant shutting down leads to the Sarah phenomenon—stress becomes burnout.

Let us look at each group as an opportunity, a chance to work with the human potential given us. When there is room not only for sympathy and antipathy but also for all the other inner gestures known to human striving, groups become exciting seedbeds for new growth. Successful groups often feel privileged to have served. Even though they may have worked for hours on behalf of the school, they will end their task by thanking the school for the chance to engage. Serving a school is not synonymous with depletion. It also can have just the opposite effect; it can enrich the personal growth of the members and give them what they could not have found elsewhere. Groups are exciting places to be. When they are well-facilitated, they provide a rich tapestry of joy, challenge, and discovery. Let us see our group work in schools less as task-bound and more as exciting opportunities for exploration.

When parents and teachers are happy with their interactions, the children know it. They see in us role models for future social life. Children want to view the world as good, beautiful, and true. They look to adults for verification of this view. They are eternally hopeful and expectant. Even when we, as parents and teachers, fall short, our children are rooting for us, encouraging us, wanting us to try again. Just as in *The Parent Trap*, the movie about two girls who conspire to reunite their divorced parents, children long to experience healing in social relationships. Schools are marvelous opportunities to provide a model for community life.

I want to conclude this chapter with a few of my favorite quotes from Margaret Wheatley on the importance of human interaction within groups:

> The dense webs of a system develop as individuals explore their needs to be together. Explorations are messy; what takes shape can't be predicted. Relationships spin out as individuals wander, negotiate, and discover the connections vital to their work. In this way, people create the structures for accomplishing the work of the organization.... The forms of the organization bear witness to how people experience one another. In fear-filled organizations, impervious structures keep materializing. People are considered dangerous. They need to be held apart from one another. But in systems of trust, people are free to create the relationships they need. Trust enables the system to open. The system expands to include those it had excluded. More conversations—more diverse and diverging views—become important. People decide to work with those from whom they had been separate.[28]

Wheatley goes on to say: "Our range of creative expression increases as we join with others. New relationships create new capacities." And finally she notes: "When living beings link together, they form systems that create more possibilities, more freedom for individuals."[29] We come full circle. From the isolated individual to the dynamics of group participation, we find that in the end our social life can enhance human freedom and create the capacities needed for school renewal.

Mentoring and Evaluation

There was once a Greek hero, Odysseus, distinguished in battle at Troy and loved by many, who, by offending Poseidon, the god of the sea, was prevented from returning home. For many a long year, Odysseus sailed about the world, the captive of forces greater than he himself. Unable to return safely home, Odysseus navigated the shoals and crosscurrents of spiritual processes, from the land of the uncouth Cyclops to the island of the enchantress Circe and the passage between Scylla and Charybdis. These outer images speak of the essential mission of Odysseus, the search for the soul:

> Sing in me Muse! Sing the tale of the man, the resourceful hero, destroyer of Troy's holy towers, sing all that he suffered, the cities he saw, the men and ways that he learned there, buffeted long on the sea, enduring it all in his heart, seeking to save his own soul, and win his companions their homeland.[30]

The quest for the soul made while struggling with the gods is the struggle to connect the divine in the human being with the world and its outer realities. Meanwhile Odysseus's wife, Penelope, and son, Telemachus, waited at home. What is home? I have moved enough to know the value of a place that is known, secure, comforting, and inviting. When at home, I am totally myself; the outer and inner "me" correspond most closely. One might say that Odysseus was subjected to physical as well as spiritual abuse in not being allowed to return home.

Once we have made the journey from our inner work to the dynamics of the group, we move into the practical realm of the classroom. If "home" is also a condition of inner life, how might it apply to teaching? In observing many teachers each year, I usually can tell within minutes of a classroom visit whether the teacher is at "home" or not. When there is harmony, security, focus, and natural ease, I can sense it immediately. Likewise, no matter how well prepared, the teacher who is not "present" will be off balance continually, will lurch back and forth, and will have a restless class. But it is not just about confidence and focus. The return home is a spiritual journey that a good teacher practices daily. In preparing to teach a lesson, one ventures forth and explores new territory but then must return within a short time to the place of origin to begin again when sharing with the students. The wider the embrace of this spiral journey, the greater will be the possibility that the teacher will be alive to the subject. Sometimes teachers need help in finding their voices, their centers, and their spiral paths of returning home with each subject. This help can take a variety of forms.

According to Greek mythology, Mentor is a friend of Odysseus, a counselor to Penelope, and a tutor of Telemachus. Mentor is willing to remain behind in Ithaca to support Penelope while Odysseus is away. When the goddess Athene wishes to accompany Telemachus on his trip to Sparta to search for his father, she assumes the form of the wise Mentor. She is symbolic of wisdom, the best way to open the secrets of the soul. And, again, it is in the guise of Mentor that Athene advises the angry kinsmen of the slain suitors to accept the inevitable and avoid civil war in Ithaca. She even turns one man into a beggar, thus divesting him of all that is transitory in origin.

For the teacher in his or her journey home, the mentor can be the friend, counselor, and tutor who provides Athene's wisdom.

These mythological images from the Odyssey yield insights on two levels. First, a mentor can have several roles. Like Athene with her different disguises, a mentor needs to be more than one person, because different people have different needs. For one, helping connect with others may be most needed; for another it might be confidential dialogue, such as takes place in counseling. For others, the mentor may need to share knowledge and help develop new skills. Thus, a true mentor needs flexibility.

There is another aspect of mentorship. The picture of Athene, the goddess of shining wisdom living in the shape of Mentor, speaks to a special quality of mentorship. The service rendered by a mentor is more than meets the eye; something greater than the person mentoring can come about if one is a conscious vessel for this work. An insight shared in mentoring is like a beam of light from Athene; it can be decisive and change the course of events. A mentor can ask, What can I call upon in order to serve?

This question, as well as the whole topic of mentoring and evaluation in schools, will be the focus of this section. Renewal in schools relies ever so much on the strength, vitality, and success of teachers in the classroom. Mentoring can improve practice on an ongoing basis; evaluation can highlight specific areas in need of improvement or help a teacher make the transition out of the profession if the needed changes cannot happen within a reasonable time. As we saw in the third chapter through the story of the teacher who did not receive the mentoring he needed, good mentoring can make the difference between the success and failure of a new teacher. Those who have received successful mentoring describe the mentor as someone who brought knowledge and life experience, who was able to reflect, who saw the new teacher's potential. The mentor respected the new teacher and could work in confidence, was good at listening and asked the right questions, set an example, took a special interest, noticed and acknowledged, was warm and generous of spirit. These and other qualities can be a gift not only for teaching but for life needs as well.

Giving and Holding Back

The giving aspect of mentoring can be easy, in that most teachers are willing to share materials, time, and sympathy. Just the fact that someone is willing to spend an hour a week talking can be a wonderful lift. The holding-back aspect of mentoring requires a more sophisticated understanding of the demands of inner discipline, for that which is held back over time and released appropriately in the course of time can become more focused and therefore stronger. For example, homeopathy uses an extract from plant or mineral substances to heal. Thus a small amount of the right medicine can heal the whole organism. In practice, this means that the mentor needs to observe fully, without trying to name immediately what is observed. If, instead of letting preconceived notions interfere, the mentor is able to let the phenomena sink in, they will begin to speak. The mentor also can observe his or her reactions to the phenomena, for they, too, will inform. If one is able to hold back from giving immediate advice and instead keeps an open space, it is possible that inspirations and intuitions will begin to work. In fact, one might say that the more you know, the more you as mentor need to hold back. Even the demeanor of a listening attitude can support reflective practices within the school. Holding back and waiting for the right moment to share can enhance the quality of the whole exchange. Of course, I am talking about hours and days; I do not advocate holding back for months what needs to be shared! Outwardly, in fact, the world may not even have a hint of the holding back, but within the mentor, the attitude of observing without naming can be an inner schooling that invites Athenian insights.

In my experience, I have found that mentors need to help colleagues distinguish between the personal and the professional. Often, professional recommendations are taken personally. We live in a time when everything is relative and subject to the feelings of the moment. It is hard for some to see that a suggestion for teaching is not a sign of personal failing. For instance, the tip that a class might work with more focus if the room were tidy does not mean that the teacher is messy, disorganized, and hopelessly inadequate! Yet such a highly personal reaction might obscure the very observation that was meant as helpful advice. In some cases, the conversation swerves into "what I meant" and "what I heard" realms instead of staying with the objective fact that some children are finding it difficult to stay on task.

In helping separate the personal and professional, it is good for the mentor to distinguish observation and evaluation. For example, rather than saying "This classroom is cluttered," which is both an observation and an evaluation, it would be better simply to say, "There are many things on the walls, some covering each other, and the shelves are so full that things fell off during the lesson." Concrete observations allow the recipient to connect on the level of the phenomena rather than immediately internalizing them with self-condemnation. This does not mean that a mentor cannot share feelings or personal responses, but this can be done in a non-accusatory manner. To the observation of the walls and shelves, a mentor could add: "This all made me feel distracted and uncertain." If one shares personal responses as observations, one retains the quality of looking at the problem together.

Judgments are particularly hard stones that should not be thrust upon the new teacher if at all possible. Ideally, after looking at the phenomena, judgments will arise within each person as a product of inner processing. When they are imposed from without, they are difficult to assimilate. There are certain words a mentor can be especially aware of, since they tend to convey a judgmental quality—always, whenever, never, must, and so on. In phone calls I have received from distraught teachers reeling from what was perceived as an onslaught of judgments, they often use such phrases as "She said I was too such and such" or "I was told there was not enough so-and-so." These phrases and evaluations lead to an emotional block that hinders the very change that the mentor hopes to encourage. The world becomes separated into those who support one (see one as one truly is) versus those who do not (are harsh and judging). Principals and self-appointed "experts" who can tell better than teach might do well to ponder Matthew 7:1–2: "Do not judge, and you will not be judged. For as you judge others, so you will yourself be judged." One way to improve school mentoring is to develop greater facility in giving and receiving feedback. I offer a few tips.

Thoughts to Keep in Mind When Giving Feedback

- Intend the feedback to help—the other person, your working relationship, and the team. Avoid temptations to relieve your frustration or anger, to get something off your chest, or to get even.

- Focus on the other person's behavior—conduct that you can see or hear. Do not make assumptions about the other person's attitudes, feelings, intentions, and so forth.

- Cite specific actions. Refrain from abstract observations and generalizations.

- Use simple, concrete language. Avoid overly complicated explanations and too much jargon.

- Use recent examples. Do not cite events and behaviors that took place weeks or months in the past.

- Be concise. Avoid long introductions and run-on reasoning.

- Be descriptive—state what you saw, what you heard. Refrain from judgmental language, guessing, opinion-giving, or reading into the other's behavior.

- Use objective language. Avoid "button pushing" words, phrases, and nonverbal signals.

- Report the impact on you and/or on the team of what you saw and heard. Avoid using language and nonverbal signals that tend to produce defensiveness or guilt.

• Pick the right time and place. Do not make public disclosures (other than within the team setting) and ensure that there is enough time to do it well and that it's a good time for the other person.

• Keep the feedback manageable. Try not to overload the other person.

• Engage the other person in the feedback conversation. Check out what the other person's understanding is of what you've tried to convey. Explore similarities and differences in perceptions. Ask what you can do to help and make suggestions concerning what might need to be done next. Refrain from assuming that once you've given the feedback, you're finished with your task.

Thoughts to Keep in Mind When Receiving Feedback

• Ask for feedback whenever you think it might be valuable to improve your personal effectiveness or contribution to the team. Avoid assuming that if feedback is not being offered, then everything is fine or can't be improved.

• Be specific about the action for which you wish to receive feedback. Avoid inviting generalizations on your overall behavior or contribution.

• Prepare to listen and to "take in" the information. Refrain from going through the motions or saying yes when you mean no about the setting, the timing, the time you have available, and so on.

• Listen as openly as you can—try "125% listening." Avoid feelings and behaviors that are defensive.

• Seek concrete, specific, descriptive examples of your behavior. Do not engage in abstractions, euphemisms, and generalizations.

• Ask questions for clarification. Try not to argue with the other person's perceptions of what was seen and heard, but make sure you clear up vagueness, abstractions, or ambiguities.

• Explore the impact on the other person or on the team of what you did or said. Avoid assuming that you know what the effects on others were.

• Summarize your understanding of what was said. Refrain from thinking that what you heard was what was meant. Check it out.

• Limit the amount of feedback being offered. Avoid allowing yourself to be overloaded with too much data or too many topics. Tell the other person, "That's enough for now."

• Engage the other person in a conversation that explores what you might do to improve your personal effectiveness, improve the relationship, contribute to the team, and so forth.

• Ask for what you need from others to support any changes you might attempt. Try not to see the situation only as your problem or issue.

• Stay focused on the feedback to you. Avoid seeing the moment as an opportunity to give feedback to the other person on something you've been harboring.[31]

Whether in Waldorf education or in public schools, mentoring needs to be seen as continuing education, a process that carries through what was launched in teacher certification programs. The mentor relationship, when effective, can stimulate self-development as well as professional growth. In my view, every teacher and administrator deserves and needs a mentor, someone who is dedicated to the improvement of school practices. To this end, it is essential that the mentor visit the classroom and observe the teacher with the children. These visits, if they are ongoing and not just in times of crisis, can become the material out of which self-reflection and growth can arise.

In the mentoring conversations, a mood of mutual learning and colleagueship is needed. This means, of course, that the conversations are confidential. It is terribly undermining to the mentor relationship if the mentor suddenly is asked to give a report to another group or to write an evaluation. If a verbal report is needed, it is best that both members of the mentoring relationship attend the meeting; if a report needs to be composed, that can be done jointly. Fundamentally, mentoring and evaluation should be separate but mutually supportive activities.

The purpose of evaluation is to take a snapshot of a teacher's work at a given point in time. This can provide an objective view of what is happening in the classroom based on agreed-upon professional criteria. An evaluator might look at the content of a lesson and whether it is age-appropriate, classroom management, the artistry of teaching, the work of the students as a reflection of the teacher's expectations, and the like. Regular evaluations are an essential professional tool. If an evaluation raises issues in need of attention, these can be shared with the teacher, who, in turn, can take them to his mentor for ongoing work. It is helpful to set up a professional development plan to address the needs, establish a timeline, and make a follow-up report. If this process is not conducted in a clear, crisp manner, a teacher can live under the vague cloud of unease for months and not know whether the process has ever been concluded. This can undermine confidence and influence the joy and enthusiasm a person needs for teaching.

In my visits to more than one hundred public and independent schools over the past three years, I have been pleasantly surprised to notice that mentoring of new teachers has improved markedly. Although further skill development is still needed, most schools now seem to take mentoring seriously, especially for new teachers. This acceptance is not always the case with evaluation, especially when it concerns administrative personnel or experienced teachers. The most intractable problems in schools arise when a senior teacher begins to falter or simply runs on "empty" too long. Often the senior teacher is a respected member of the school community; he or she may even have a position of responsibility in the school but for some time has not been growing professionally. This is a particular issue with teachers/administrators in Waldorf and other schools that practice site-based management, namely, the senior teacher who gives much attention to administrative work and has little "juice" left for the children. Roles need to be changed periodically, and colleagues and parents need the courage to speak up when the children are benignly neglected.

Sometimes a school becomes like a large family, with all the benefits and some of the drawbacks. One difficulty in working with evaluation in such a family system is that the problems of a teacher are embedded in the very fabric of the school. This means that specialists might be hired to augment the deficiency. I even have seen committees and structures created around a problem teacher. Out of close working relationships, a kind of mutual dependency can be formed over time, which hinders objective evolution within the system. For this reason, I strongly recommend that every school supplement peer evaluation with outside evaluators. It is hard for a peer to step out of the family dynamic and risk the ire of a colleague by naming a problem. An outside evaluator or evaluators can better raise consciousness and most often is listened to more attentively.

Finally, there are several aspects of our work in schools that apply to both mentoring and evaluation:

• Observations are not enough. My son once had a teacher who passed every evaluation and observation, and the paperwork that resulted did not document any serious concern. Matters were far from satisfactory, however, when the observer was not in the room. In the end, the parents of this Waldorf class demanded a change in teacher under the threat of leaving en masse, and the teacher was not rehired.

Evaluations need to include parent interviews, conversations with administrative personnel, and unannounced visits.

• The mentor or evaluator needs training to see more than meets the eye. It is helpful to put on "lenses" to look at the lesson from different perspectives. For instance, one can view the whole morning from the perspectives of sympathy and antipathy or from the auditory versus the visual. Or one could focus on initiative: Is the teacher the one to initiate everything, or do the children have support for initiative? Is the teaching concrete or abstract? Who is working at each part of the lesson? Is the teacher doing it all, or are the children expected to participate? One could look at the morning from the point of view of transitions. How are questions worked with? Who participates and when? It is a wonderful training for the observer to take a theme and use it in several classrooms over time. Thus, mentoring and evaluation can become action research.

• Realize that the teacher may share a presenting issue in asking for help. But that presenting issue may mask a core issue that needs to be uncovered. We tend to look at symptoms more readily than we find the causes. Mentoring can help schools dig deeper.

• The mentor or evaluator needs to remember that we all have preferred ways of seeing the world and that self-awareness helps us overcome bias. It is good to frequently check in with oneself: Am I bringing an assumption to this lesson? Are my preferences playing into what I am seeing? Are there things I admire more than others; if so, do they influence my recommendations?

• Are there issues here that go beyond a particular teacher, issues that should be addressed by the whole school? If so, how can the mentor bring this issue forward so as to support the overall learning environment of the school?

• The mentor and evaluator need to know the difference between professional development and basic teacher training. There are times when one has to refer a teacher to others, rather than begin a tutorial.

• It is helpful to "remember together" what happened in the lesson. As soon afterward as possible, go over what was experienced. In remembering together, you are equal. This review also creates a climate of safety in which more exploration can occur. The goal of the mentor is to bring the teacher to say what needs to be changed. This awareness becomes the agent of real growth, the impetus to become a good teacher. The mentor can help but then must step aside in respect for what only the teacher can do out of personal initiative. There is a saying in the Gospel of John (3:30) that works well with mentoring: "He must increase, but I must decrease."

As with all adult interactions, it is best to mentor out of lived experience, rather than abstractions. Using images and concrete examples, the mentor can help a colleague see things afresh. Simply looking at the right phenomena does much. If looked at clearly, they will begin to speak. In addition, a teacher's dedication to the children will assist in taking up the changes that are needed. This heartfelt energy in our schools should never be underestimated.

7

LEARNING GROUP SKILLS

Stages of Group Development

Now that we have considered the spiritual aspects of connecting with others in the journey of renewal, we move toward the practical aspects of working in and being part of a group. It is helpful to notice how much of our time we spend in groups. Some are formal situations, such as meetings of large and small groups, committees, conferences, retreats, spontaneous administrative problem solving, study groups, and professional courses. Particularly with the increasing availability of technology, people seem to gravitate toward group events as a human balance to sitting in front of a keyboard. With rare exceptions, most people have extensive interaction with groups of various types and sizes. How we use this opportunity for a sense of real community is our own choice.

Given this reality, it is not enough to look just at the individual dimension of school renewal and what each of us can do in our separate journeys toward renewal. One aspect of renewal must be considered in terms of the group and how the group functions. In fact, I have observed that an otherwise successful and healthy teacher or parent can be worn down gradually by a dysfunctional organization. The patterns of human behavior affect how we breathe, think, talk, and interact. To understand this idea from the negative aspect, all one has to do is look to the nearest group of teenagers and see the effect of peer pressure in their lives. On the positive side, a self-aware, proactive individual can influence the dynamics of a particular group, just as the culture of an organization can influence the work of each and every teacher. Much more attention has been paid to the curriculum and teaching needs in a school than to the issue of organizational health.

Just as human beings change and grow over time, so, too, do groups. Most of us acknowledge human changes, especially those related to childhood. It matters to parents and teachers alike if a child is three, six, or nine years old. Our responses differ depending on the age of the child. Less noticed are the changes that take place in the life of a group. Sarah felt the subtle changes in the faculty at her school over the years, but she was too busy to stop and observe what was really happening, let alone do anything about it. When Sarah's school went into crisis, everyone wanted a solution to the immediate problem, yet there were few individuals available who were active in training, skill building, and learning about group dynamics. Without an alignment between "tasks" and "competencies," a school tends to use mostly Band-Aids. A more fundamental approach is needed in our schools.

By looking at the stages of a group, each of us may see ways we can encourage active and successful groups. The following descriptions are based upon the work of Blanchard Training and Development in San Diego, California. This organization has developed various assessments and training models that have helped me in my work with schools over the past few years. Using their materials and the experiences of my colleagues at Antioch New England Graduate School, I describe five typical stages of group development.

Orientation

Try to remember what it was like when you recently joined a new group. You may have felt considerable enthusiasm for the task or project at hand; otherwise, you would not have made the effort to attend. You may have anticipated a positive outcome or felt the need for the work, yet at the same time it is likely that you experienced anxiety and concern about your role in the group. Who are the other people around me? Will I fit in? Do they share my hopes for this group? You may remember looking to the leader to see what would happen first, and you may have needed reassurance that everything was well-planned and considered. You may have felt relief at seeing an agenda and having time for small talk. This stage of group development can be characterized as having low to moderate task accomplishment as the energy of the group is focused on defining goals and tasks, exploring a possible approach, and using skills that participants have brought from previous situations. Orientation that acknowledges and works with these dynamics can build a good foundation for future group work.

Dissatisfaction

It is quite natural for a group to pass through a stage in which participants feel frustration with the lack of progress and focus of the group. It may be that members experience the discrepancy between their initial expectations and reality. It could become apparent that members have different expectations altogether or that assumptions are exposed and the purpose of the meetings is questioned. At times during this stage, people can feel varying levels of incompetence and confusion. It is also characteristic of this stage in group development that members may have negative feelings toward the formal leader or other members who are perceived as assuming informal leadership roles. The group seems to call out for strong leadership, yet members at the same time can feel unhappy with their dependence on authority. In their unhappiness, they often become more dependent on whatever leadership is available. Overall, the work of the group at this stage is interrupted continually by the need to process negative feelings and mixed expectations.

Resolution

Eventually, most groups begin to work things out. They start to resolve differences, reaffirm goals, and focus on the tasks at hand. Members become less dissatisfied as new ways of working together become clearer, with the result that negative feelings toward other members and the leader abate. As feelings of mutual respect grow, trust is developed, and out of the new feeling of harmony, members are able to use more fully the human resources of the group. As a result, the accomplishments increase, and individuals feel greater satisfaction, which, in turn, influences self-esteem. This positive cycle becomes self-reinforcing as positive feelings grow. Along the way, new skills are acquired, and members gain fresh understanding of both the content and the needs of the group.

Production

At this stage, one has the sense that things are humming along, work is being accomplished, and the members feel good about their participation and the eventual outcome. Members are working well together and seem to agree on the nature of their relationships. Now more autonomous, they do not depend on the formal leader but can support situational leadership as it emerges. As part of this mature phase of group development, members recognize, support, and challenge one another's competence in a way that draws out the talents needed for the task at hand. Members communicate openly and freely without the fear of rejection or conflict, for their energies are focused on task accomplishment rather than on resistance or dissatisfaction. They also are able to relate to each other in terms of complementary task functions as well as giving interpersonal support. Thus, the meetings are enhanced by pride in tasks well done and the cohesion of the team. Members thrive as they learn and develop new capacities.

Closure

Frequently, too little attention is paid to the final stages of a group, and members simply rush out the door. Closure is important as a way of winding down, sharing, learning, and making new skills conscious so that they can be applied to the next assignment. It is also natural for the last stage of a group's work to include a certain amount of letting go, sadness about ending, or feeling of a lack of focus. Sometimes the impending separation hovers like a cloud, and members try to obscure their feelings of separation by joking, missing meetings, or throwing out tangential comments. At closure there is usually still considerable feeling of accomplishment, yet there is a sense of the need to move on. Naming this stage and engaging in review will help all participants let go with a feeling of completion. Some consideration of follow-up and reporting also are needed during closure.

Life becomes interesting when one looks at the changing leadership styles needed for these stages of group development. There are many ways to consider this linkage, but one aspect is the degree of support versus direction needed by a group. Supportive behaviors include asking questions for clarification, encouraging participation, asking for amplification, affirming, confidence-building, and helping members participate fully. Directive behaviors on the part of a leader can include setting goals for the meeting, going over the agenda, calling on members for input, chairing the discussion so as to stay on task, and wrapping things up clearly and succinctly.

When a group is in the orientation phase, it needs leadership that is restrained in support and strong in direction. People want to know what is happening, and they look to the leader for direction. Wouldn't it be awkward if, at the first meeting, the leader just sat back and socialized? The dissatisfaction stage might arrive earlier than usual! When it occurs, the dissatisfaction stage calls for leadership that is strong in both direction and support. One might say that of all the cycles of group development, this second stage requires active, energetic leadership. Unfortunately, the opposite is often what happens. When faced with dissatisfaction, a leader will step back aghast, and that response only worsens the problem. What is needed is a leader who understands the dynamic, supports the members, and continues to direct. I often have said that at this stage, it is almost better to take any direction with a task rather than abdicate movement altogether. Dissatisfaction is a way in which a group begins to ask more of its members, and it is not the time for the leader to take a break.

When resolution sets in, however, leadership can continue to be highly supportive, but less direction is needed. Encouraging, guiding, and supporting, the leader no longer has to run the show. Finally, in production, the leader can give both little support and little direction without affecting the work of the group. In fact, I have seen a formal leader leave the room at this stage without the group so much as noticing. It is just as important for a leader to back off at this stage as it was for him or her to expend energy in earlier stages. Closure, in my view, requires a hint of all modes of leadership—summarizing, support and direction, and a sense for wrapping things up so that life can move on.

For me, leadership is a response to the needs of the group, not an imposition on the group. In fact, when a leader lags behind, that is, continues to adhere to a style the group no longer needs, the members at first covertly and then overtly will resent the leader. There is nothing worse than leadership that retards the growth of a group. This may sound absurd, but I have known schools founded by a strong leader that flourished for many years, only to go through a period one could term the "dark ages" when they outgrew the founder. Old forms, like old habits, can be an iron lung that hinders the healthy breathing of the social organism.

Rather than viewing the stages of group development described in the chapter as linear, one might best see them as a spiral. There is constant movement from one stage to another, and just as closure is reached, many members may be moving into the next situation that will require orientation. Having worked with this model for a few years, I would like to offer a few tips on keeping things alive.

First, when a new person joins a group, there is a natural regression of at least one stage. That means that a group in the resolution stage may find itself moving back into dissatisfaction if the new member is not able to integrate easily. Awareness of this tendency to slip back could help if the leader, and indeed the membership, could take the time for a conscious, if abbreviated, welcoming through orientation. The entire group is new with the addition of a new member.

In my experience, many groups handle orientation in a perfunctory way. This might mean going around the circle with brief introductions or reading the agenda. I suggest that if more attention could be paid to orientation, the dissatisfaction stage might not be so debilitating. For example, orientation is not just about task orientation but also about process and group maintenance. How are we seated? Does everyone feel comfortable? Is there enough light and air? Where are you in relation to this meeting? What issues and concerns do you carry that might influence our discussions? The more these things are made explicit at an early stage, the less they will work insidiously into the conversations later.

Moreover, many people hold their leaders suspect, give them a short leash, and then criticize them for not doing more. If a group can share expectations of leadership before the work begins, the person in the role of facilitator can know what is wanted and expected. I am particularly concerned with the "short leash" phenomenon, in that few people then agree to serve, and those who do serve often feel unsupported. Popular culture is full of fear of the tyrannical leader, but in schools, I find this is rarely the case. Instead of the tyrannical leader, I find tyrannical groups that hold a kind of impersonal sway over the life of the school. Whether it is called a committee, board, faculty, or college, a group can create culture in which no one dares take on leadership that is innovative, creative, or inspired. When leadership is faceless, parents despair. The "we have decided" becomes a form of escapism in which no one is accountable, yet everyone has an oar in the water.

As an example, I am often frustrated when my son's school simply announces a change in schedule with the proclamation "The faculty has decided." In yearning for an ego—a single presence or a face—with whom to interact, I sometimes seek out a teacher with a question or a request for explanation, and the response is typically another well-worn answer, "It was decided." Where is the ownership? Why the need to hide behind the wall of the group? This failure to allow individuals to speak for a group can lead to frustration and a hierarchy within the school community. I long for the kind of leadership that speaks with these words: "The faculty researched various alternatives and as an active part of the process, I decided to lend my support to this solution because…." Every adult in a school is a leader. Let them speak!

Leadership also needs to be self-aware and creative in gesture. This means that self-knowledge and personal development can free a leader from the confines of personality and allow true service. Strong, decisive leadership on behalf of a school can be a good thing if it is done in true service. The artistry comes in the implementation. Just as a painter can feel when the red needs a hint of blue, so also a leader must work creatively with the human talents available in a school community. Connecting the right people, arranging events that foster community, speaking privately with a colleague before an issue blows up, using a sense for timing in facilitating a meeting—all this and more constitute the art of leadership. If we can move beyond the command-and-control military model and adopt an artistic model for leadership, we will have gone a long way in showing how schools can transform social perceptions.

Finally, as stated elsewhere in this book, when there is doubt, I suggest that leaders bring situations into movement. There have been times when I have been utterly at a loss as to what to do, and everyone expected something. Rather than assuming that the answer would come in the form of a concept, I have found that bringing matters into movement almost always helps. So when I do not have a clue, I often simply ask a question, begin the dialogue, get things started. The solution usually is hiding somewhere in the group, ready to pop out when no one is looking. Movement brings life, and life teaches all.

Separation and Return

Being part of a group also requires that we look at the group consciously. In doing so, take a few moments to step outside the group and gain new perspective, just as I walked outside the cathedral at Chartres and saw it differently. Most parents have the experience of sending a child off on a trip, perhaps to visit grandparents or to attend summer camp. These short-term separations can be difficult at first, more so for the parent than for the child, I find. If the choices were well-made, there is the compensatory feeling that the distance is good for the child, and, of course, the return is usually known and anticipated. In fact, time away can even strengthen the relationship, in that we all need to be reminded occasionally not to take one another for granted. How they appreciate our cooking when they return from camp! The return from these minor outings can engender much sharing, not only about the events that have transpired but also on a deeper level. As a father, I have experienced some of the best conversations with my children some days after their return from such an excursion. My oldest son and I often end up taking a walk, going to the gym, or just chatting in the car, and those conversations usually have more breadth and scope after he has been away.

Separation and return can enhance the principle of growth and give both parties a renewed sense of confidence and security.

For instance, it is wonderful when a family can return to the same vacation cottage each summer. One arrives with a sense of anticipation, rediscovers old scenes, and relives the past while experiencing the present with fullness of heart. Coming back year after year is a life-giving rhythm that allows for spiritual growth. Just look back to similar experiences in your biography, perhaps a recurring festival, trip, or family tradition. The reconnection is both outer and inner; one's spirit is renewed.

The theme of separation and return also can be harnessed to bring the energy of renewal to groups. If group meetings simply take the same configuration week after week, it is like living in the same house year round without ever taking a vacation or experiencing a change of scene. Most schools adopt a favorite meeting format and then stick to it. In public schools the staff might meet in the library, with teachers behind desks and the principal in front trying to conduct business as efficiently as possible to minimize the time required for the session. In a Waldorf school, the meetings are often held in a classroom with chairs drawn into a circle. There is no wrong or right way to meet, but the dynamics at play within the meeting are most important.

Using the notion of differentiation and integration can enhance the health of our meetings. As with the family vacation, this is a process that holds enormous possibility. Differentiation can take place on several levels, but it might be as simple as breaking up into smaller groups to work on an issue. The small groups allow for more intense conversation and engagement and, at the same time, alter the dynamic inherent in the large group. Differentiation also can be an inner process in which the participants look at one aspect of a problem, taking it apart before putting the pieces back together. Integration is the return, the bringing together from all sides. This might be simply the return of small groups to the large gathering, or it might mean integrating groups that are separate in position, such as parents, teachers, and board. The process of integration creates a sense of the whole.

In my experience with schools, differentiation is the more prevalent of the two processes. We tend to feel most comfortable meeting just as teachers, for instance. For the most part, we know where we all stand. It always seems to take extra effort to arrange and conduct a meeting of mixed groups, and the stress level seems higher. This is unfortunate, because when the principle of differentiation is supreme, old habits and tendencies can govern the emotional and cognitive processes unconsciously. Meeting as a cohort group can be life-supporting but also can become life-endangering.

One of the reasons that people resist integrating separate groups in a school is that the assumptions, norms, and meeting expectations are not clarified, so people can feel adrift in an integrated group. For instance, meetings of only teachers tend to develop a protocol, a way of working that carries the members from one week to the next. This means that the members learn to expect a certain way of opening, a process of facilitation that works, and a sense of purpose that unites the teachers. When thrown into a mixed group, all bets are off. Sometimes the results confirm the participants' worst fears: One parent or teacher might monopolize the time, the members may have different agendas, and the expectations may vary so much that no matter what happens, some will walk away unhappy. All one needs is a few unsuccessful mixed group meetings to confirm earlier prejudices. The feeling arises that the real work of the school can happen only in a specialized group.

This need not be the case, however. If one gives the care and attention to the needs of a mixed group, one can experience a wonderful explosion of creativity and positive energy that radiates out into the whole school. To begin with, it is helpful just to recognize that the needs of the group are different when the membership is drawn from various components of the school. Thus, one needs to spend time aligning expectations and goals, clarifying the purpose of the meeting, establishing norms of meeting conduct, and actively facilitating. In fact, I find that the more diverse the group, the more active the facilitation needs to be. By contrast, a well-worn group of colleagues who have met over the years know one another so well that they need little facilitation. The established working group can function because the members know one another so well, yet that same familiarity can result in a family dynamic in which the connections also serve to perpetuate dysfunction. People in the group have learned to work around certain problems. These problems may then go unaddressed for years. In fact, many people unconsciously transfer meeting habits from one setting to another, only to be rudely awakened when things don't work so smoothly. This awakening can happen when someone changes the meeting format, setting, membership, or style of facilitation. Integrating mixed groups has the effect of bringing to the surface that which has been ignored; it is a way to promote honesty in human interactions.

A school can experience renewal if meetings, and indeed the school as a whole, use the qualities of both differentiation and integration. From the differentiated groups, such as the teachers meeting, one can achieve in-depth insight, continuity of purpose, and the understanding needed for developing curriculum that is responsive to the needs of the children. This becomes a rich underpinning of the school. From the integrated group meetings, one can broaden the perspective, enlist new resources, and test closely-held assumptions. When working together, differentiation and integration can become a creative process, one that spirals upward in an organic manner, leading the school to constant replenishment. What is learned in a differentiated group can be experienced in a new light in an integrated group, which, in turn, leads to fresh insight when one returns to the differentiated group. If one watches how a plant sends forth leaves, one can see the collecting up and sending forth as a spiral dynamic. As with the processes of growth in nature, differentiation and integration in schools can enhance growth.

Separation and return also can be experienced on a deeply personal level, through a crisis or major life change that becomes the impetus for individual growth. When there is such a life event, the school as an organization cannot do much, but compassionate colleagues and parents can help hold the person in crisis. A death in a family can send ripples throughout the community, but the full impact of the event is experienced most by those with a heart connection. Colleagues and parents often overlook the lingering impact of such a major event, and the successive waves that wash in months, even years later. Because these matters are so important in the picture of renewal, I would like to develop further the individual dimensions of separation and return.

The scene was Abbot Hill Road at the intersection of High Mowing and Pine Hill roads. Returning from dropping off my son Thomas at High Mowing school one morning several years ago, I passed my ex-wife driving onto Pine Hill with Ewen. His sweet face was peering out the window, and for an instant his round eyes gazed directly into mine. We met for a moment, and then the cars passed on. I would not see him again for several days, until the next visit. Tears streamed down my face as I drove on. My son, younger brother of Thomas, the one we had all wished for so long, was out there, passing me in another car. Missing him at breakfast, at play on the living room floor, throwing a ball in the yard, and reading a bedtime story rushed in on me again. How could the world be so cruel? My heart ached.

For a second or two the logical, reasoning side of me tried to enter in, saying: "In order to spare Ewen conflict, you agreed early on in the divorce process not to have a custody battle over him and to support Thomas in his wishes. This is what you agreed to." Logic carries little weight in matters of the heart, however. A father missing his younger son needs to embrace the sorrow. Rather than explaining or even understanding this situation, I wanted something deeper. I wanted this to teach me, work in me without a predetermined outcome. And it did.

Time has passed, and Ewen and I experience more joy than ever in our times together. The moments once taken for granted we now engage in with a new fullness. For example, bedtime stories are usually not possible in the evenings, except every other weekend when he is with me overnight. There was literally a gap in reading as well as an abyss of the soul. I experienced "nothingness," an empty space, and I could so easily fall into the void and the separation. What to do? After some experimentation, I found another way. On afternoons with Ewen, we started reading just before supper. It was different—he was not wearing his pajamas and had to get in the car and leave afterward—but after a few minutes on the sofa, we entered into the story, and everything else disappeared. We were enveloped in the activity, and activity nourishes. I had to find a new way while holding true to the ideals I carry as a parent.

Separation and return are a modern fact of life. Things that are living cannot just be strung out further and further over time. One cannot grow a plant simply by collecting a bunch of separate cells. Change in one form or anther happens to us all. The question is what we do about it. In my case, and I suspect for many men, my old response was to just barrel ahead, move on without looking back. And there is value in moving on, but in the moment, I have found it best to embrace the reality, even if it is not always pleasing. The further I lived into and really experienced the dynamic with Ewen, the more I was able to access new layers of myself. And the unexpected result was that becoming more whole myself did more to help us than anything else I could have imagined (including finding my new wife and soul mate). Renewal is thus not just a matter of meeting skills and organizational change. It is also a deeply personal matter.

Finally, I will say a few words about regret, which is a frequent by-product of separation. It is so easy to set high ideals for oneself, ideals that in many cases cannot be achieved. Many teachers plan lessons and goals that are difficult to achieve in the time allowed. Relationships at home and in school can fall short of the ideal. The honeymoon of the first year at a school as a parent can give way to disillusionment later. Wherever ideals are not realized, the possibility of regret sets in. Just as the original ideal can create new life forces, so the regret can slay the life of the spirit. When a pattern of regret is established, it can be corrosive.

A former colleague, who has since passed on, shared a touching story with me some years ago. She told how in preparation for Christmas, she had stayed up very late for many nights making gifts for the students in her class. They were received with great joy on the last day of school before vacation. Then, just two days later, Christmas arrived, and she realized she did not have any gifts for her own children. She had to rush out to buy things that were much less than she had hoped to make herself. For weeks and months afterward, she regretted having put so much time into her school gifts and so little into her family's Christmas. Now ill with cancer, she sat across from me and spoke about the many regrets of her life. She said, "It was my regret and guilt over the years that brought me to this illness. Now at least I can face the issue. I have waited my whole life for this."

One will always feel inadequate to many of the tasks at hand, and not everything can be fulfilled when we want it. The important thing is striving for a balance between the ideal and what truly can be achieved, to make those daily living choices with clarity and then embrace them in fullness. Not everything is possible today or even in two days. Transitions take time, and one cannot live just in the past or the future. The present is now. How do I live with this thought, with this feeling, with this moment? There needs to be a kind of breathing between the ideal, such as the Christmas presents, and the reality of the time needed to make them. We are all traveling faster than ever before, and it is so easy to lift off a bit from the ground of existence. When we do, we tend to continue moving in the same direction, giving more time and energy to some things than they deserve. Each task calls for a different level of energy, of life force. It is respectful of the people and things around us to know what is required and not to give too little or too much. Also, staying grounded and connected to the smallest daily tasks is a natural corrective. I find great solace in weeding, washing dishes, and placing things in order around the house and yard. There is the immediate satisfaction of seeing the results of one's work right away, of seeing the change.

Change requires letting go of whatever holds us back. A person can build only on the positive actions he or she takes, on what is a living seed in the soul, that which has divine blessing. Renewal cannot be built with the broken stones of regret. Rather than wishing one had done better, one might hope to do better in a similar situation in the future. Can I be awake next time, see with new eyes, and be there in a different way when I meet the next challenge? This is a productive use of remorse, if it encourages the will to do better next time. Regret is a narrow view of life indeed. In regret, one can be self-centered and oblivious to the greater workings of the cosmos. To what end are my struggles? At the threshold of life and death, one might ask the questions "How did you help me carry my cross?" and "How did I help you carry yours?" This question takes us beyond self-help to the essential human task of our time. And in relation to one another, in joining with others in this way, we achieve a new perspective. Life itself is a separation and return—a separation from our spiritual home at birth and a return at death.

Framing

> We each create our own worlds by what we choose to notice, creating a world of distinctions that makes sense to us. We then "see" the world through this self we have created.
>
> —Margaret Wheatley[32]

What we create in the way Margaret Wheatley speaks of becomes a lens through which we see, interpret, and seek new information. The information we seek serves to validate our previous views, thus leading to a self-serving, circular system. Consequently, we frame issues and problems by how we tend to view the world. It is as if we each have an individualized mental map that guides us in our daily navigation. These maps, or theories, can create differences in reality. Often with the best intentions, people act out of their beliefs or "mind maps," and these actions form the social and organizational situations in which we live.

When things go well in a school, these self-made worlds are not challenged. And things often go well just because of the synchronicity of many individuals meeting in an exciting venture designed with the hope of creating a better world for our children. This spirit of hopefulness, plus the special grace that comes from working on behalf of children, can allow many different people to work together despite their different "worlds" of inner reality. The children serve as powerful agents of cooperation; they help parents and teachers find common ground. The early years of a new school are marked by such a special period of grace, in which the positive will of cooperation is paramount.

Sooner or later, the wake-up call arrives, typically in the form of a challenge in the external reality of the school: It might be a change in administration, finances, hiring, or evaluation or even just an issue in one particular grade. When the wake-up call sounds, the different frames of reference held by key individuals are highlighted. Suddenly, people realize that they do not see things in the same way. Challenges that arise as a result of the wake-up call help us see the different viewpoints of the school population. In our journey of renewal we can meet these challenges in the group arena and learn ways of listening, speaking, and facilitating. A challenge for many schools is enrollment, since it is directly tied to funding and income. This issue and others like it can expose the areas in which the school as a whole does not function well. One can recognize the areas of challenge or disharmony in the way the different groups within the school community frame the issue. Four possible ways to frame the same issue are given here. Let's say that the enrollment in the seventh grade has fallen.

A board member's response:
Yes, I remember well the meeting last spring when we were deciding how to allocate resources in the new budget. Some wanted to start an after-school program, others hoped to raise salaries, others were pushing for a new language position, and still others wanted us to replace the furnace. Each group was represented on the board, but it seemed that the particular projects had the strongest advocates, and the needs of the faculty as a whole were neglected. So we deferred the salary increases and put off adding funds for professional development. No wonder the teacher we hired for seventh grade is struggling. Wouldn't you struggle if you worked nights at the local grocery store?

A teacher's response:
Yes, enrollment has fallen, which is not surprising given the parent dynamics in that class. Quite frankly, I am relieved that some have left. They really had it in for the last teacher. Our new colleague at least will be able to count on supportive parents.

A parent's perspective:
Yes, the class has grown smaller this year, in part because of the way in which the new teacher entered the school. I remember well the first day. I know he had just moved into his new house the night before, but he arrived late for the opening assembly and seemed to hesitate before joining the other teachers on stage for the yearly introductions. His jacket was rumpled and his tie awry. He seemed really out of it. For me at least, that moment was symbolic.

An administrator's response:

Yes, the enrollment has fallen in that class, owing in part to the committee system we still have in place. While most were away this summer, the personnel committee continued to interview candidates for the position. But as it turned out, no one on the committee had middle school experience. They finally found this untrained teacher, hoping he would take courses over the summer. Little did they know that the professional development funds had been cut, and besides, he wasn't able to move until just before the start of school. The last teacher had really had a rough time, you know. Many parents simply left in the vacuum created after the resignation. Even after the new teacher was found, the announcement did not go out until late July, because the faculty chair was on vacation. We really have to examine our committee structure.

The same phenomenon, namely, the drop in seventh-grade enrollment, elicited four different responses. The administrator used the structural frame, looking to the way in which committees hire, fire, and communicate. The parent used the symbolic frame, one that affects us more than we realize. The assembly was a defining moment for that parent and perhaps for other parents; once an image is created, it persists, as McDonald's and many large corporations know. The symbolic frame works more at the unconscious level and can surprise us with its strength.

The teacher used the human resource frame, seeing the issue as a matter of people interacting with one another. The parent/teacher dynamic is spoken of frequently among teachers and can be the preferred way to understand an issue. The board member quite naturally looked at the problem from the political/economic frame, seeing the issue as the result of competing interests that play through the budget discussions. In the end, according to this frame, there are winners and losers, and those who successfully advocate and build coalitions will prevail. Of course, a board member might use the human resource frame, just as a teacher might see things from a political or economic perspective. The point is that individuals have preferred ways of viewing the world. It is best not to negate these differences but to use them constructively for the benefit of the school.

Rather than having a four-way conversation among the individuals, a facilitator might name the obvious and ask that each person share a perspective on the seventh-grade situation. Simply calling for different perspectives frees the situation and lifts it out of the "I'm right, and you're wrong" dynamic. Once the perspectives have been shared (and one might hope for more than four), a skillful facilitator might ask: "What did you learn from the other perspectives?" This places the emphasis on learning and interest, rather than position and argument. It is part of human nature to want to learn and help; people are interested in people.

The next stage of the process might be to ask: "Given that we agree on the issue, namely, that enrollment has declined in the seventh grade, what have we learned that could help us use the talents represented here to increase enrollment?" The emphasis here is on common ground, that place where there is agreement rather than contention. And, second, the facilitator is challenging the group to use their different frames to reach a cooperative solution. Usually the group is in a good place by this point, and the solutions come fast and furiously. "Let's have a middle school fair." "How about the publicity? We could have parents contribute letters to the local newspaper." "Let's be sure to include professional development funds in the budget next year." It is surprising how quickly the group agrees on the commonsense solutions to the problem, once the energy has been redirected and the separate frames are used as resources rather than obstacles.

Finally, a step that is neglected frequently in the euphoria of brainstorming and the feeling that the meeting was better than anyone expected, the facilitator could ask: "Given what we have learned, how could we replay the process to arrive at a better place next time?" This element of reflection can ground the learning and increase the chances that what that group went through can be transferred to the next situation, which might not look at all like the last one, on the surface. Teachers work with transference of experience in the classroom, but the adult learning community often rushes on to their respective busy lives and forgets this last stage. This "replay" can happen in the group and also individually, for there are lessons that each might tuck away for future use. Eventually, if the learning is valued and shared, parents, teachers, administrators, and board members can reach a stage of freedom in which each member can choose to see a problem from one frame or another, depending on the needs of the school. It is a wonderful experience to hear the following:

From a teacher:
I see how that first-day assembly must have been symbolic for those parents and friends who had not yet met the new teacher. The faculty has examined the issue from the point of view of the human dynamics, but is there some-one here who can help us with the structural perspective?

From a board member:
I am glad to hear of the work that has gone into the sev-enth-grade issue on the part of the faculty. What I hear is something that had not occurred to me. Our admin-istrator is in a good position to see the layout of the school committees. Let's ask her to join this conversa-tion before we go any further.

Simply knowing that different perspectives exist can shape our language and attitudes behind the words that we use. Often people use code words or words that can be "hot" for one person but not for another. This sets off small fire alarms internally, and people then resort to negative language and forms of behavior. When we have done inner work and our language is at least neu-tral, it invites the best participation from others. The final words of the board member are particularly telling; they recognize the fact that someone else can do something better. We have moved from a self-centered world to one in which there are other people who together can do more than I can alone.

Affirming Decisions

Understanding the importance of framing issues can lead us to the best ways to reach decisions in a group setting. A decision is a form of free human action. When a human being actively searches out and grasps a concept or intuition, thereby bringing it into full consciousness, a self-sustaining decision can arise. Individuals, not groups, make decisions.[33] Where do decisions come from? For me at least, they have a mysterious quality. It is hard to determine what is really happening in the moment in which an individual makes a decision. There is certainly an important element of preparation, but the second in which one realizes a decision there is a magical element at work. There is an intuitive quality to the act, and intuition is connected to the will, the motivational aspect of our constitution. It is as if we dive into the lake of decision and really know what we have come to only a split second after we emerge on the surface. Decisions are bigger, more encompassing than we realize, and our consciousness grasps just a portion of what was really at work in the act of deciding. Each person in a group goes through a slightly different process; usually, one person *surfaces* with a decision, and others in the group *recognize* the validity of the decision and affirm it. Much confusion occurs in schools and groups that do not understand the nature of decision making. Blame, hurt, isolation, and social pressure can result from the inability to perceive what is truly at play when decisions are at hand. Experienced at first on a personal level, a teacher or parent may gradually lose trust in the group, and the community suffers.

One of the great myths that surrounds decision-making in many Waldorf schools is that consensus is the only way to work and that the inner circle has a lock on all things spiritual. This becomes a lethal combination that can create self-enclosed groups that have the aura of esotericism, thus becoming unapproachable, mysterious, and seemingly superior. The difficulty arises when the surrounding community observes the quality of decision-making and realizes that those participating in the inner circle are less than divine. Often a crisis in confidence ensues, such as the suspension of the student in Sarah's school, with much painful learning on all sides. Those parents and teachers who have been through a few of these crises become wiser, learn to work together over time, and see that it is best to enlist the striving intentions of all adults who wish to serve the best interests of the children.

As we have seen, there are also casualties along the way. Teachers grow tired of endless meetings and withdraw to their own classrooms. Parents get fed up with the general dysfunction experienced in decision-making and communication and either leave, or just opt to support their child's class and not participate actively in all school events. Either way, the school looses vital human resources. I suggest that a school seeking renewal spend time looking at the nature of decision-making and find ways to differentiate between the types of decisions needed in various situations. For example, one might look at the following possibilities:

Unilateral decisions are the ones needed when there is an emergency, when there is little time to gather a group, when the task at hand is clear and universally recognized.

Majority decisions can be helpful when a procedural issue needs to be resolved and the group is unwilling to spend the time on a minor issue, such as the starting time of an open house. Some may want it to begin at 1 p.m. on Sunday and others later in the afternoon. Either way, the event could work well, and a simple majority can make the decision so that more important planning can be done. In the end, it is better for the school that a decision is made rather than waiting to the last moment and leaving too many people mystified or confused. A majority vote also might be taken when the group has spent enough time on an issue and some wish to give over the decision making to a mandate group.

Mandated decisions are those that are entrusted to a smaller group that will act on behalf of the whole. It is important that the *whole* group knows what the mandate is ahead of time and that the assigned group is trusted to do the required job.

Consensus decisions can bring a collection of individual decisions to a place of mutual recognition. This can be an exhilarating moment in a group; there is a sense of unity that is precious and sometimes fleeting but well worth the effort with the right group. I have found that consensus as a way of decision-making works best in the following context:

- The group has stable membership.

- The group meets regularly, that is, once a week. The rhythm of meetings exercises more influence than most realize. The weekly rhythm works well with a highly conscious approach and is needed to support the interconnection necessary for consensus decision-making. The weekly meeting cycle thus works more with that part of us that returns in full consciousness over time, whereas monthly meetings are more connected to the cycles of the life force that work in and around the people participating.

- The group is not too large. I prefer groups of five to twelve, but I have experienced groups as large as eighteen to twenty-four that in certain circumstances achieve real consensus.

- The members of the group are committed to the long-term development of the school or institution.

- The members of the group share a common spiritual striving.

This description of consensus from M. Scott Peck describes the delicate nuances involved:

> Consensus is a group decision (which some members may not feel is the best decision, but which they can all live with, support, and commit themselves not to undermine), arrived at without voting, through a process whereby the issues are fully aired, all members feel they have been adequately heard, in which everyone has equal power and responsibility, and different degrees of influence by virtue of individual stubbornness or charisma are avoided so that all are satisfied with the process. The process requires the members to be emotionally present and engaged; frank in a loving, mutually respectful manner; sensitive to each other; to be selfless, dispassionate, and capable of emptying themselves, and possessing a paradoxical awareness of the preciousness of both people and time (including knowing when the solution is satisfactory, and that it is time to stop and not reopen the discussion until such time as the group determines a need for revision).[34]

One way to foster renewal in schools is to practice honesty with regard to intentions. Do we intend to be a group of the type described here? If we are, then are we willing to put in the work required? If not, can we find alternatives to consensus that we can live with?

It annoys me when these questions are not addressed and a kind of hypocrisy creeps in. We pretend to work with consensus and studiously avoid the fact that we are not working out of a shared philosophical basis. "We are all entitled to our own spiritual practices, after all." Likewise, our commitment to the group changes, depending on personal needs and interests. So I attend some meetings but not others, hoping to express my opinions regardless. Schools then wonder why they are not successful, why salaries are low, and why education is not respected in the community. In my view, it is better to have an enlightened leader than dishonest group processes.

One phenomenon in most schools is that even if one group in the school can say yes to the cited criteria, other groups, by definition, cannot. Most parent groups, for instance, will not be able to meet as regularly as the teachers, limit the size of the group, make the same commitment, and achieve such commonality in terms of spiritual striving. Yet schools need active parents. A central question then becomes: Can we be flexible enough as human beings to adapt our membership skills and leadership styles to the needs of the group? In other words, can we let go of ideals that cannot be met by the reality of situations? To answer the needs of the group with flexibility becomes a matter of collaborative leadership. Let me point out here that mixed groups, that is, groups of parents and teachers and other combinations, provide a resource that is far from realized in most schools.

A final thought on the misuse of consensus: There are times when the attempt at consensus, however well-intentioned, can have serious side effects that often go unnoticed at the time but have long-term repercussions for the health of the school. Because it is often socially unacceptable, or personally repugnant to *block* a decision, the effect can be to silence an individual's misgivings or drive them out of the meeting into less productive channels of communication. In the worst cases, this kind of individual silencing leads to a kind of repression of true feelings and the expression of opposing thought. As we saw in Sarah's story, a teacher who has felt the social pressure to conform can leave a meeting with knots in the stomach and much to unburden at home. Over time, personal health can suffer, and the home fabric can become frayed. What is not tended to at school is often transferred to the home, eroding preparation and, over time, marriage and family joy.

Some groups pretend to work by consensus when, in fact, they use alternatives that are thinly disguised. (I have found this to be true in some Waldorf schools.) Here are a few examples:

- Majority rule. When we see where most people stand on a particular issue, we will force the decision through using the adjournment time or any other rationale to make the minority acquiesce. Often those in the majority do not even know that there was a sizable minority view, and the insights of the few were not able to improve upon the will of the majority.

- Unilateral decisions based upon the unspoken hierarchy. This way of working takes the form of having a discussion until one or two particular persons speak up, at which time the different perspectives that were in the room suddenly become *one*. The effect is that some people carry more influence than others. To have influence is not necessarily a bad thing, but when it is obscured under the guise of consensus, it is a real social injustice. It would be far better to say: "We will have a discussion on this topic until our senior colleague or faculty chair feels he or she has enough information to make a decision on behalf of us all."

- Decisions that are made by groups that are not mandated, outside the context of the regular meetings. This is the form that most infuriates me. There is a general meeting with general discussion on a topic. There is no closure or indication at the end of the meeting about what will happen next, but in the intervening week a decision *appears*. It remains unspoken that a small group met, without the sanction of the whole, and made a decision. If the decision is questioned at the next meeting, the response of that small group will be: "You are not being supportive of your colleagues." Who wants not to be supportive? In this way, the issue is twisted; instead of being rightly viewed as a gross violation of group process, it is contorted into an issue of support. Many conclude after a few such experiences that it is best not to rock the boat—"Let others handle those administrative matters," they say. "I'll just focus on my teaching."

Thus periodic review of how everyone is doing can redress and balance what is not well. I have found that groups in a school need to hold each other accountable, with minutes that are freely circulated. It is best to write down clearly who was in attendance, what the issues were, which decisions were made and how, and which items were slated for action, along with specific names of the people who are meant to follow through. At the next meeting there must be a review of the decisions, with the expectation of a high standard of performance. To say that there is not enough time is not a valid excuse if tasks are neglected repeatedly. Setting priorities on a monthly basis can be helpful, so that the group is making decisions out of the larger picture. With regular care and tending, a school can adopt the forms of decision-making that respect the reality of the groups within the community.

8

LEADERSHIP AND COMMUNITY

Parent Evenings

We have come full circle in our journey of renewal and are ready to further our inner journey by working with the larger community through leadership. In this chapter I want to focus on the educational and community-building aspects of school renewal. Both can play a significant role.

Most schools have parent nights of one sort or another. They may be schoolwide events held in the auditorium or individual class evenings hosted by the teacher of a particular grade. These evenings are often informative, intended to share announcements or describe the school or aspects of the curriculum. Teachers usually are willing to share their knowledge and experiences with parents at class nights. These evenings can help parents understand the curriculum, elucidate aspects of child development, and build a foundation for school programs. When they are carried out successfully, a teacher will use anecdotes, humor, and an assortment of lively activities to engage the interest of parents. It is ever so important that parents recognize and support what is happening in the classroom. They can then do more to follow up at home and know when and how to communicate with teachers. In my experience as a parent, class nights can be both fun and informative. No two teachers do things the same way. Every parent wants to know how his or her child relates to the curriculum. It is also great to sit at a little desk and look through the assortment of official and unofficial documentation inside.

When a school takes the class nights seriously and urges that parents attend or inform the school if they are not able to be present, then many potential problems in the parent-teacher relationship are alleviated. Issues that could become serious are dealt with in an informal, small group rather than in phone chains or in the parking lot. An accessible teacher invites parents' questions and helps parents feel safe. Most of all, an emphasis on education-based parent nights can lift the issues out of the personal and into an objective reality of developmentally appropriate curriculum. The question "Why is my child like this?" becomes instead "How can I work with the teacher to meet what we are both seeing?" Parent involvement has proved to be one of the best indicators of student success, and parent nights can energize and focus everyone.

Other aspects of these parent evenings are often not as developed as the knowledge-based approach. One example is what I call the community-building aspect. Yes, most schools have refreshments, encourage questions, and engage in conversation during parent nights, but that is merely the tip of the iceberg. I would like to focus on a much more aggressive aspect of community building. In ancient times, educational leaders were priests and persons of high authority in society. For example, the pharaoh in ancient Egypt had complete rule, not only over the laws of the land but also in the regulation of work, construction, and the annual flooding of the lands around the Nile. The word of one individual held sway over the lives of millions. This is, of course, no longer true today, and there has been a separation between political leadership, which is invested with outer authority, and religious and educational leadership, which relies mostly on persuasion for legitimacy. Teachers struggle to win respect in the larger community, yet when they are in the classroom (especially in the younger grades), they often are revered and respected as in the old priest culture. It is the teacher who holds sway over the riches of history and the secrets of science and mathematics. It is the teacher who has the final word in matters large and small, from the answer to the multiplication problem to permission to be excused to go to the restroom. In the classroom, the teacher is an authority, and there is nothing wrong with that.

The problems arise when that queenly/kingly authority is exercised in the parent-teacher relationship. Yes, there is an arena where the teacher needs to be the dispenser of wisdom, sharing the curriculum and so on. But for community-building to occur, I maintain that other dimensions need exploration. When the teacher is the *wise priest* sharing the elements of the curriculum, he or she is in a directive mode. This works for a teacher most of the school day. In a gathering of parents, a teacher's supportive rather than directive role can be a balance and can enhance the quality of group work. By "supportive" I mean encouraging participation, asking questions, paraphrasing what has been said, asking for others to comment, and so forth. These communication techniques draw the parents forward and make sure that what needs to be said is said in the meeting or later in private conversation, rather than elsewhere. In a successful parent evening, a teacher balances direction and support.

Many of Sarah's colleagues worked very hard at preparing stimulating lessons for their students and enjoyed steering the ship of their classes through the day. But when they gathered together as colleagues, it was sometimes as if the ship had too many captains and not enough sailors. Goodwill often got them through collegial difficulties. They always tried to embrace and support each other as best they could. But this same approach did not work as well with the parents, who needed more than the teachers seemed to be able to give. At a class evening, Sarah's colleagues held forth for as much as an hour, talking about the curriculum and the wonderful things that the students were doing in school. The teachers were also strong advocates of social values, such as limiting TV watching. The problem, especially in Sarah's absence, was that the parents were given too much direction and not enough time to process what they were hearing.

One skill that I have found immensely helpful is that of combining inquiry and advocacy. The authority figure is often good at advocacy: "Let me tell you about all the wonderful things we are doing in school and how much time and effort we have put into our work." In this mode, the parents listen—it is hoped with respect—but they are absorbing more than processing. As with nutrition, intake without digestion can lead to problems. Symptoms of too much directive energy I have observed are these:

- Absenteeism. "We have heard enough." These types of parents tend to avoid class nights, or sometimes only one parent attends from a sense of obligation.

- Internal judgments about what is acceptable or not in terms of sharing opinions and questions. "This teacher clearly has strong views; it might be best if I not rock the boat or jeopardize my child's position by crossing that line."

- Passivity. "I will be there, but I don't want much more asked of me. If I do anything for the class or the school, I will choose safe things, such as baking cookies or driving on a field trip. It is best to avoid speaking my thoughts and feelings, because I am not sure how they will be received. For the most part, I will remain passive."

- Making the distinction between rapport with the teacher and acceptance of the philosophy of the school as a whole. "My child is happy and safe here, but since I have not fully processed and thus not understood all that is said about the curriculum, I will let that be and just be a helpful parent." In my experience, this is a big problem in some independent schools. The parents may support specific activities of their child's class but not the school as a whole. Without shared vision, it is difficult to have a *whole* school community.

• Conflict between mothers and fathers, often along the lines of those who attend the class nights and those who do not. For those not often present, a few early impressions can take on undue importance, and the communication gap between mother and father, parent and school widens.

• Finally, when the priest culture is too strong in a school, one tends to see parent involvement with particular classes but not on schoolwide projects, fund-raising, or capital campaigns. You need community for buildings to materialize.

Rather than just practicing advocacy, a good mix of inquiry can be crucial. To inquire is to question, ask, probe, investigate, express curiosity, and learn more. Lead questions include these: What do you think? What was happening for you? What was your experience? How did that occur? In this sort of engagement, one is asked to suspend judgment, avoid cross-talk, examine assumptions, be self-reflective, take risks, and seek out deeper meaning. Teachers and parents can benefit from this kind of inquiry.

In our Collaborative Leadership Program at Antioch, we use a training exercise for learning to balance inquiry and advocacy. With a skilled facilitator, it can look like this:

• Groups of five or six people are formed.

• One person is chosen as a point person—someone who wishes to work on an issue with the group. An example might be to look at how to increase the level of trust within the school community.

• The group engages in a process of inquiry only—asking, not telling. The point person may respond verbally.

• Everyone is asked to stop, and the members of each group write down their assumptions: What are the assumptions you hold about what you are hearing and experiencing?

• The group continues the inquiry while suspending assumptions. At this stage, the point person does not respond verbally. He or she may want to ask another group member to take notes, so that the point person's full attention may be paid to the group.

• Now the group begins advocacy. The group engages in advocacy only, stating views or giving advice. The point person may respond verbally but should listen carefully to what is being offered.

• The group now tries to balance inquiry with advocacy, with everyone participating.

• The group can conclude by reviewing the exercise together.

In many different settings, I have found this exercise both demanding and transformative. People look at things differently and use new skills. Community-building happens before their very eyes. A balance of inquiry and advocacy can have the following effects:

• Support individual and group learning.

• Create open communication.

• Teach us to suspend judgments.

• Clarify our own meaning and that of others.

• Help move people beyond individual understanding.

• Enable us to change our mental models.

• Allow individuals and organizations to achieve a higher level of creativity.

Facilitation

I have attended many meetings over the years—too many, in fact. Some have been worthwhile, while others seemed to take place because that was the thing to do at an appointed date and time. Once you give space for a meeting, that space will be filled. For this reason, I rarely have sympathy for those who want more time for meetings in order to solve problems. People learn and find stimulation in a group setting, but meetings alone can never replace the personal transformative work that really moves the agenda.

Of course, the way in which a meeting is conducted depends much on the leadership of those responsible. This leadership can take many forms, such as chairing, minute-taking, or facilitation. When I am in a meeting that is chaired, I experience the personality and human intentions of the chair in terms of the agenda and how he or she leads the group through the issues. A chair is often *directive* in the sense described earlier. There are specific goals that need to be met, and the chair tries to move a group, sometimes through persuasion, sometimes through the force of personality. A chair is usually the focus of attention and sits in a central location with clear authority for the conduct of the meeting. A facilitator is someone who serves the process more than directs it and has a different way of working.

There is much literature on facilitation, and I will simply highlight a few helpful techniques and the importance of skilled facilitation in maintaining the health of groups within a school. "A facilitator helps the group realize that sustainable agreements are built on a foundation of mutual understanding."[35] Thus, the facilitator helps people learn and strive toward insight that could not be gained singly. In pursuit of mutual understanding, the facilitator encourages full participation, fosters inclusive solutions, and helps create an environment in which people can develop new thinking skills and take risks on behalf of the whole school.

Most groups carry assumptions about what is acceptable and what is not acceptable in terms of new ideas and risk taking. In exploring these assumptions, I always am amazed at how restrictive people are in what they think will or will not be accepted within a group. In other words, many people box themselves into narrow bands of acceptable communication, limits that are self-imposed out of old habits in human interactions. A facilitator, through the practice of the art of group process, can expand or stretch the limits (see illustration) and help members dig deeper and reach further through such means as:

• Paraphrasing. This is essentially a listening skill in which the facilitator uses his or her own words to say what has just been said. This can confirm the essential ideas, support the speaker, and keep the discussion on the topic at hand.

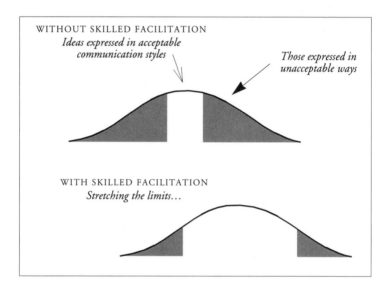

• Drawing people out. Here the facilitator gives a member encouragement to air views before a decision is needed. Often some members hold back too long and then speak at such a late date that it appears they are holding up the decision. A good facilitator will notice this and draw out silent members early on. Also, there are times when the facilitator knows that key information is not on the table. It is essential that the information be available to everyone early on.

• Mirroring. More exact than paraphrasing, this technique captures the exact words of the speaker. If some members have not been attentive, or a key issue or question needs to be addressed, mirroring can help make sure that everyone is on the same page.

• Gathering of ideas. This method is used in large groups and at conferences, and can help people focus on the task and become involved. I find that it can be overused, however, and can lead to indigestion. Much is put out in terms of brainstorming, and at the end the members ask themselves, "What happens now?" The lame response is that the material will be collated, minutes taken, and so on, and often one never hears anything more. Healthy digestion requires time for processing as well as consuming.

• Stacking. This method takes the form of a deli, where numbers are assigned to the many people who want to speak, and they are then free to relax their hands and minds and listen to those speaking, confident that each will have a turn. This technique works in large groups, but if it is used exclusively, it can limit real conversation—the back-and-forth exchange of ideas in which new thinking is developed. It is a *safe* facilitation technique that is used when the facilitator is fearful of losing control or might not know the membership.

• Tracking. We have all participated in discussions in which it seems that several themes are being addressed at once and members become confused about the subject at hand. With tracking, the facilitator names the different conversation themes, decides to pursue one for a set period of time, and promises to take up the others next. This helps the members give themselves fully to one topic.

• Encouraging. This technique speaks for itself.

• Balancing. This is one method I wish were used more in school discussion groups. A facilitator uses balancing when he or she draws out the opposite point of view. Steiner once said that if one thing is true, the opposite also may be true. It is an excellent discipline to examine things from several viewpoints. Too often, groups assume that the main reason for meeting is to agree, the sooner the better—if we agree on my terms, even better. The rush to agree inhibits full exploration and closes off possible inspirations. Also, when groups rush to agree, positional strength can be given greater influence than insightful strength. Those with titles and formal authority are given more influence, even though the most helpful idea could come from the most unlikely person. A facilitator can help by drawing out opposite points of view with neutral language. "Could anyone here characterize the opposite point of view?" Or, "Have we considered this issue from all points of view?" If this is done before a decision is reached, the group finds itself anticipating objections and questions that would have come from members of the community. By balancing viewpoints while matters are still held in the group, things can be worked with constructively rather than defensively afterward.

• Intentional silence. This is a technique the Quakers have used effectively for years. Silence lets people dig deeper. A good facilitator will allow this to happen. I recently attended a Quaker wedding, in which I experienced the beauty of intentional silence. People spoke when they were moved, and yet the spaces between were even more eloquent. The silences honored my own inner processes and helped me stay centered and at peace with myself. Silence can help me increase, whereas too much talking diminishes my inner resources. A facilitator can tap greater possibilities when silence is allowed to work within the group.

• Finally, a facilitator tries to listen for common ground. Is there an area in which we agree? Why not put aside some of the minor differences and articulate what seems to be common ground? Not everything can be settled at once. I think that it is best for a school group to find common ground and move forward, rather than dithering for weeks because some people have problems with a few aspects. Do what can be done, and the action will give renewed strength to tackle future challenges.[36]

I have observed that many schools select chairpersons, not facilitators. As mentioned earlier, chairing a meeting is much more *directive*; it has more of a corporate board feeling. Often the chairperson is the one with greatest formal authority, which often impedes real dialogue. I suggest that if a school needs to select a chairperson to represent the work to the larger community, then the internal conversations should be facilitated. This may require training, but it is something that any parent or teacher can learn. I have thoroughly enjoyed some of my sessions at Antioch, where almost anyone can step forward to facilitate a meeting. This gives the organization tremendous flexibility in managing human resources. As with the breathing system in the human being, facilitation enhances movement through the intake of needed replenishment. A meeting that is well-facilitated can be like a concert; one walks away feeling satisfied and refreshed.

Leadership

Anyone who takes responsibility for a task can exercise leadership. This means that in a school, virtually every adult is a leader. This needs to be articulated in the school's organizational structure and communicated as an invitation for initiative. Rather than place too much emphasis on the single person, whether it is the principal or the faculty chair, this definition of leadership creates the possibility of true collaboration, a theme that I develop at the end of this chapter. First I would like to characterize two less positive appearances of leadership found in many schools, aspects that in many cases hold back organizational development and the forces of renewal.

The Reluctant Leader

We probably all have been there. It is a meeting in which there has been much discussion, and now, toward the end of the afternoon, it is clear that someone has to take on the task that has been articulated so assiduously. There is silence. Eyes begin to drift furtively around the room. In the pregnant pause, many questions and comments flit through the minds of those present: Who will take this one? Who is acceptable? Not so and so! What can I say to influence the outcome? My plate is full. Who will speak up first? Someone then mentions a name, and all eyes move accordingly. Perhaps a few other names are brought forth. Then, perhaps with more or less discussion, one person is asked, cajoled, persuaded to take on the task. Often reluctantly, someone ends up taking on the job.

With variations, this story repeats itself again and again. Those who take on leadership roles are often hesitant. Why? We have many talented people in our schools who want to serve, and some are even eager to take a leadership role. Why all the reluctance and hesitation? Partly it is the process. Large group selection with the candidate present is an awkward format, one that does not always foster initiative. But there are other reasons as well.

Many adults in our schools grew up as part of a generation that was anti-establishment, anti-war, and, in a way, anti-leadership—as visible in politics at least. They have leadership images of the military *command-and-control* method of leadership, including third world dictators. Out of this mindset, many adults today have rejected leadership that is invested in the individual and have a strong preference for working within groups. There is safety, anonymity, and moderation in groups. Given such fixed, outdated views of leadership, many prefer the chaos of leaderless schools and endless meetings to the rigors of reinventing attitudes toward leadership.

Another, often more tangible cause of hesitation in leadership is the phenomenon of unsupported leadership. Everyone can remember when someone took on a task and worked hard at it, only to have it shot to pieces when it was brought back to the group. Many people like to avoid taking leadership roles but clearly reserve the right to criticize, amend, or change what someone else has done. A kind of tyranny of the majority arises in which no one dares to step out too far ahead of the perceived majority opinion.

One result is that people are more reluctant than ever to take on leadership roles; those who do are afraid to take risks. As with any organization that does not take risks, such a school hinders growth and can stagnate easily. I can smell this kind of stagnation within a few hours of being in a school. A stagnant school might be well maintained, classrooms may be orderly, and the teachers may be doing their work. But stagnation creeps out under the doors, through the hallways, and into all the adult gatherings. It is a school in which form and structure are greater than pure excitement, in which the unspoken rule is that "we do things this way." The people do what is required, but not much more. Participation is minimal at voluntary events, and roles are well established. Although titles and committees may change on the surface, in a stagnant school one finds that basically the same people are in control year after year. The patterns of behavior are entrenched. Darwin rules—by a process of natural selection, only those who fit in are attracted to the school's leadership structure, and others are weeded out eventually, either by leaving or by being marginalized. In practice, the latter is apparent when a marginalized teacher or parent says something and the meeting goes on as if that person were invisible.

When I was conducting a workshop in a public school in Maine some years ago, I was amazed at the lack of response from the group. I failed to connect—they were so passive. After an hour, someone was called out of the meeting, and the group came alive. They were real teachers! They asked questions, raised issues, and participated with creative problem solving. Later I asked why things had changed so dramatically, and I was told, "When Jack was called out of the room, we were free to be ourselves." Jack, it turned out, had been the principal for many years. His ineffective leadership style gradually had discouraged initiative throughout the school. Everyone was waiting for his retirement.

As a civilization we frequently are outspoken, and rightly so, about crimes committed in third world nations, the homeless, and teenage violence, but who is prepared to speak out for the many schools that are dysfunctional? Many of the organizations that could serve as the sources of renewal in our communities are stagnant bastions of the very establishment that many purport to reject. Our institutions become ever more conservative as they age; by "conservative" I mean staying with what has worked best in the past or that which requires the least effort in the present. A teacher who might have been energetic and reform-minded when beginning to teach could come to emphasize, over time, that which maintains control and harmony. We end up liking to do what we have always done, following the well-trodden paths rather than blazing new ones. In this conservative, often stagnant environment, no wonder we have reluctant leaders.

The Volunteer

At the end of a board meeting, the chairperson asks whether there is anyone who could emcee the all-school meeting. In a Waldorf school, this kind of event happens at least once a year and serves as an opportunity for reports, orientation, questions, and discussion of schoolwide issues. Most people in the room know that this will be a difficult community event, one that will require a leader with a cheerful disposition and considerable skill at facilitation—someone who is good at soothing ruffled feathers. A certain parent volunteers, and everyone groans inwardly. This is the one person least suited for the job. She is hopelessly disorganized and yet likes to be at the center of everything. There is silence. The chairperson asks, "So, I guess we are all set?" More silence. The parent nods, and the all-school meeting is off to a dubious start. Actually, a hint of sanity returns through much-behind-the-scenes jockeying in the ensuing days. The role of emcee eventually is shared, and the school has learned to work around problems.

What did not happen, either at the board meeting or in the days that followed, was any forthright conversation with the volunteer. The board itself did not have a way with which to deal with volunteerism. No one wanted to take on the person in question, and so the whole school had to absorb the issue. Because we are always grateful when someone will do the work free of charge and because the needs in a school are so great, we often fail to have the same clarity about roles and responsibilities that we have in hiring. We then have good people who end up suffering from the modern malady called "boundary ambiguity." Volunteers can be left wondering, "Where does my task end, and how do I avoid stepping on someone's toes?" This lack of clarity can lead to frustration and less inclination to volunteer in the future. Volunteers need to see concrete responses to initiatives, or they will not want to donate time again. One parent said to me, "I will never serve on the [board] enrollment committee again. Every time we came up with a new idea, it was sent to the faculty and changed. When it was returned to the committee, it bore no resemblance to the original impulse. But then they wanted us to implement a plan that none of us could relate to."

This issue of volunteerism has an inner aspect that informs the outer realities played out again and again in our meetings. The people who congregate around schools bring an assortment of talents, things that they have accomplished in life, but most people I know also have a strong desire to develop new capacities. In a school meeting, it is the latter that often speaks more strongly. It is as if an inner voice says, "Volunteer for that which you hope to become, so that you will develop as a human being." Rather than selecting a task based on past accomplishment, many adults volunteer for endeavors for which they are least suited. The school ends up with good-hearted people who have volunteered for the wrong tasks, the ones they are least able to do. The community then has to bear the consequences.

Volunteers are essential to schools, but they need to be managed; professional standards are just as important as with employees. If this is not the case, the volunteers themselves will burn out with frustration, and a school will have to hire people for tasks that could have been done by parent volunteers. Professional standards include basic common sense in selecting a leader: a clear description of the job, discussion concerning the qualifications desired, a process of selection in which several names are solicited, and a committee to sort them out and make a recommendation to the board or another decision-making group. Professional standards also include feedback along the way and celebration, or at least acknowledgment, of a job well done. The free donation of time needs to be respected all along the way. At each stage it is good to ask for reaffirmation of time commitment, which also opens the door for clarification of boundaries. It is helpful if a review can be completed afterward, so that the decision makers can do even better in their selection process next time. In this way, a school becomes a learning organization not just for our children but for all that serve.

The Disguised Dictator

Few people would tolerate outright dictatorship. It is anathema to a democratic society. With just a little alteration for the sake of appearances, however, I have found dictators lurking in the hallways of our schools. It is risky to characterize only some appearances of dictatorship, because there are many. In my experience both in public and independent schools, the disguised dictator typically is someone who has refused in recent years most formal leadership roles or has stayed with the few that have worked well in the past. The disguised dictator usually is a senior teacher who wields authority beyond his or her present role as a classroom teacher. The strength of the dictator's position is revealed not so much in what is said in the meetings but in what happens after the meetings. Mysteriously, what was discussed one way can end up being implemented in another way. Sentences, even entire paragraphs, seem to vanish from letters to the community, or else a crucial addition is placed in the letter that somehow changes the entire emphasis. A disguised dictator, of course, will speak up at meetings, but often toward the end of the discussion and in a way that tends to bring matters to an abrupt conclusion.

The disguised dictator also can be a school board president or a major donor in a private school who wields extraordinary influence and is not afraid to exercise it. I knew a board president who was quite congenial during meetings and actually ran an effective board, only to walk the hallways the week after, grabbing key people and applying subtle pressure. Here was someone who had authority that exceeded his formal role, influence that was greater than that which was given by the school.

One antidote to the disguised dictatorship in our schools is to begin to support situational leadership, creating a culture that allows for leadership when a person with a particular talent or capability is needed. Not everyone can do the same things, and when we support those differences and even rejoice in the talents of others, we start to break down old patterns that sustain dictatorship. Perhaps more than anyone else, a dictator knows how to play the system. Change the rules, bring in a new dynamic, and the dictator is disempowered. There is no better antidote to stagnation and dictatorship than collaborative leadership.

When this is not entirely possible, I have suggested simply naming what you observe. This might mean taking an occasional risk in stating what everyone else is experiencing, such as, "It seems that the group has accepted Janet's view. If that is the case and no further discussion is needed, we should acknowledge that and move on." Gradually, over time, others in the group may take courage and take on the disguised dictator, who may herself not be entirely comfortable with her behavior patterns.

The Servant Leader

In his book *The Journey to the East*, Hermann Hesse tells the story of a pilgrimage undertaken by a secret organization called the "League." The servant Leo, who accompanies the caravan, is described in this way:

> He helped to carry the luggage and was often assigned to the personal service of the Speaker. This unaffected man had something so pleasing, so unobtrusively winning about him that everyone loved him. He did his work gaily, usually sang or whistled as he went along, was never seen except when needed— in fact, an ideal servant. Furthermore, all animals were attracted to him. We nearly always had some dog or other with us which joined us on account of Leo; he could tame birds and attract butterflies to him. His desire was for Solomon's key, which would enable him to understand the language of the birds.[37]

Later on, the narrator, one of the pilgrims on the journey, has a conversation with Leo in which they discuss how some artists often appear only half-alive while their creations seem to grow in significance and vitality over time. Leo then says:

> "It is just the same with mothers. When they have borne their children and given them their milk and beauty and strength, they themselves become insignificant and no one asks about them anymore."
>
> "But that is sad," I said, without really thinking very much about it.
>
> "I do not think it is more sad than all other things," said Leo. "Perhaps it is sad and yet also beautiful. The law ordains that it shall be so."
>
> "The law?" I asked curiously. "Which law is that, Leo?"

"It is the law of service. He who wishes to live long must serve, but he who wishes to rule does not live long."[38]

At one point in the journey, Leo disappears. As a result, the narrator, unable to find him again, wanders off and spends years in great misery and self-doubt. By accident, he finally finds Leo again, makes awkward conversation, writes an impassioned letter, and finally ends up following Leo to a meeting of the League:

And again, as I did many years ago when I watched him and the way he walked, I had to admire him as a good and perfect servant. He walked along the lanes in front of me, nimbly and patiently, indicating the way: he was the perfect guide, the perfect servant at his task.[39]

At the end of the book, the narrator discovers that Leo is in fact the president of the League (the leadership organization) and that the journey was as important as the goal. The failure was not on the part of the League but on the part of the narrator, who was not able to follow. True leadership, in Hesse's view, is a service, and to serve means to exercise self-knowledge.

In the quoted passages, one finds many clues to the notion of servant leadership. I find the descriptions of Leo helpful, such as his ability to work cheerfully, be there only when needed, and serve as a guide to help find the way. The whole discussion about art and creating new life is fascinating. As a mother or father with children who may well grow to be far more than their parents, the leader is an artist whose work is more important than the position itself. When it comes to leadership in our schools, these insights can be the bridge between dictatorship and headless anarchy. Yes, we need leaders, but they are there to serve, not to command. And the best guide walks a path that leads to something greater, a vision that all can embrace.

Robert Greenleaf, author of numerous books on leadership, speaks of the kind of participation that can generate shared vision:

Can the leader accept that optimal performance rests, among other things, on the existence of a powerful shared vision that evolves through wide participation to which the key leader contributes, but which the use of authority cannot shape? ... The generation of a shared vision may be one of those things that just happens when genuine respect for persons, for all persons, is consistently manifested."[40]

This language may be persuasive, and many readers might agree. The difficulty is that many of our schools are built upon the principle of authority, which rightly belongs in the teacher-child relationship but often is misplaced in the adult community. When it is a matter of creating community around a shared vision, no one person, founder, or philosopher has the exclusive rights to that vision. Gone are the days when education and mystery teaching were reserved for the select few (see The New Community). All who truly seek can find. When schools try to become a community of adults, participation is like the sap in a New England maple tree. It can ebb and flow, but its movement is the life of the tree. Sever that flow, and the process of death takes over. Given the right nutrients—a culture of trust—the life of a school can flourish.

Collaborative Leadership

If every adult in a school who takes responsibility for a task is a potential servant leader, the crucial issue becomes how we can best work together. We begin with examples of serious challenges. Most teachers are prepared to work with curriculum, understand child development, and enjoy supporting the process of learning in their students. Fewer are trained or prepared in terms of meeting facilitation, conflict resolution, and communication with parents or administration. As we saw with the story of Sarah, the "other side" of school life can be overwhelming, even for those who are capable. Parents bring a wealth of professional and life experience but often little experience with school administration. So we have two groups of adults—teachers and parents—who are pulled together by the children but who have little preparation for the work of the school. Although things often turn out amazingly well, owing to the goodwill and commitment of everyone concerned, we cannot wonder when things get crazy as the result of the diverse backgrounds of those called in to work on behalf of a school. It is as if one were to ask an electrician to raise vegetables or a dentist to paint portraits. At times, parents and teachers are all intent on tasks for which they are not adequately prepared.

Rather than giving up in despair and disbanding or hiring an expert to fix everything, there is a more exciting possibility, namely, collaboration. By working together through mutual insight and recognition of talents and hindrances, it is possible to enlist the best from all community members. There are several possible stages in the collaborative process that can be used for any task or group:

- Outreach. Early on, it is good to look at the potential of the task. Who should be part of this work? Who needs to be here? What are we hoping to achieve? The wider the scope of consideration at this stage, the less likely there will be problems later on. In my experience, most mishaps take place in the area of communication and the omission of key people early on in the process.

- Cooperation. At this stage, groups have been established, and they have articulated norms, that is, understandings about how they wish to be together. At the level of cooperation, the various circles of activity exist side by side.

- In collaboration, those circles begin to merge. Because there is an exchange between people and groups, one can feel energized and have a greater understanding and a sense that things are alive.

• Finally, a new structure or accomplishment is reached in which the various groups no longer feel separate but are part of one whole. As one moves from the first to the fourth stage, greater levels of trust are created. People are willing to open up, grow, and change as personal shadows are pulled out of the corners and new light is cast on the striving of participants. A greater sense of security through collaboration allows for new initiative and risk-taking.

A group that is tight and well-formed and has consistent membership—that is, the "inward" group—needs to be particularly conscious of reaching out, again and again. In contrast, a group that is already diverse and far-reaching in terms of varied membership and focus needs to work inward again and again, to share but from a centered, balanced place. The one-sidedness of each group is amended by the qualities of another group. If we strive to reach the whole child in our classrooms, it behooves us to look at school issues from the viewpoint of the whole as well. Rather than continually retreating into safe committees, which often serve simply to reinforce the established views of its members, it would be better if groups could move in and out of the stages of collaboration on a regular basis. In this way, they gain natural correction and new energy through the processes of life. Living organisms breath, circulate, and collaborate. Why not schools?

One way to make collaboration a reality in a Waldorf school is through eurythmy in the workplace, a form of movement that allows for much exciting group development. These carefully developed and sequenced movement exercises combine experience, reflection, and conversation in such a way that the participants visibly experience fundamental issues of leadership, cooperation, decision making, and transformation. Preconceived notions dissolve, and people experience one another anew. Difficult knots of human interactions, past and present, gradually are untied, and new relationships are formed. Going beyond just talking and conceptualizing, eurythmy liberates and frees that which seeks to find new expression. Non-Waldorf schools should consider an appropriate group activity that involves the same kind of physical connections. All collaborative leadership training needs the art of movement!

I would like to summarize the key thoughts in this chapter once again by way of a verse by Rudolf Steiner, one that can accompany a leader in the path of self-knowledge and service:

> May wisdom shine through me
> May love grow within me
> May strength penetrate me
> So that in me may arise
> A helper to all humanity
> A servant to all that is holy, selfless and true.[41]

At the Gates of Heaven

As part of a training program, I once asked a group of teachers, administrators, and interns to describe the leadership qualities most needed by our schools today. Despite all the challenges faced by our schools today, they were able to articulate remarkable attributes that embrace both the reality and the ideals inherent in leadership service. They felt that a leader is one who

- Can look at his/her own life and honestly admit to personal shortcomings while always striving for an ideal.

- Is able to step back, observe, embrace, and know those who follow.

- Works with the strengths of others and acknowledges and encourages leadership in others while also perceiving weaknesses that allow for proper delegation of tasks—thus is a realist.

- Recognizes the spiritual as well as the pragmatic leadership needs of a group.

- Cherishes the word, which goes farther than the physical places we travel; tries to think/consider before speaking and always attempts to include kindness and gentleness in his or her words.

- Has a heart that is big enough to carry others.

- Can reconnect with the natural world and the life forces that provide the source of inspiration.

- Can find the individual in the midst of a bureaucracy.

- Can put human relationships ahead of everything else, because in the end it is the quality of those relationships that makes everything possible.

- Forges partnerships with others, is able to enhance cooperation.

- Needs to respect the other person even if that person sees things differently.

- Needs to respect himself or herself so as to respect others.

- Inspires confidence, because you can lead best if others have confidence in you.

- Is able to perceive and work with diversity, can see the cultural and biographical background of individuals so as to weave a rich tapestry.

- Gets out of the way so that others can work with his or her contribution, because leadership and genuine authority come from modeling your behavior, intellect, and imagination and then allowing others the space to come forth .

- Is able to learn from mistakes and move on.

- Is able to look at his/her behavior in light of personal ideals, for there may be discrepancies at times.

- Is a master of devotion—if you lead, you need vision, an all-embracing heart, and moral technique.

Finally, those who have served speak of the threshold experiences that come when one is a leader. These threshold experiences are not just the big ones, that is, death and birth. They also occur in innumerable ways daily. Experiencing the threshold is like standing in a stream. A leader often stands where the current is most swift. Much passes by that others might never notice. But by virtue of standing on that ground, the leader must brace his feet, lean into the current, and accept what comes floating by. Often the task is more that of redirecting things rather than taking them up and trying to solve them, but leaders working with threshold experiences are more than glorified traffic cops. They often have the honor of hearing, listening, and being brought into personal stories that can enrich the soul if they are carried properly. Many of our schools are invitations for meetings, personal interactions, and resolution of history that is far more complex than meets the mortal eye. A leader at the threshold is able to bear witness to these life struggles.

With the new consciousness of our time, one can experience much in small, seemingly insignificant moments: a conversation, a wrong turn on the road, a chance meeting, or a decision to take up one task or another. These threshold experiences lay the soul bare; they reveal us. There is a moment of illumination, of self-awareness, of being in the hands of the Other. The countenance of the leader at the threshold is both severe and compassionate. The severity comes from the power of the natural forces at work, the inevitable current of time. There are experiences that must be lived, which are full of pain and carry us further whether or not we wish to go. But there is also kindness and compassion in the face of the true leader, for inside is the knowledge that all these experiences can, and do, happen to them as well. Leadership is not an exemption. With upright bearing and a gaze that takes in both the far and the near, a leader stands like Peter at the gates of Heaven.

The New Community

After identifying social and historical phenomena in this section, I would like to highlight several practical ways in which human beings working in the context of a school can begin reforming community to meet the demands of our time. I will end with a few final words on Sarah and sources of inspiration that helped her school heal and move forward.

Our schools today provide a meeting place for two converging streams in human evolution: the individuation of the human being and the lessening of group consciousness. These emerging evolutionary trends can be demonstrated by a thorough study of history. For the purposes of this text, I would like simply to observe that the human being, once an integral part of the whole, gradually has achieved greater and greater freedom to act, think, and feel as a separate entity. As we have seen, in ancient Egypt and other early civilizations, the human being was completely bound up with the social unit. In Greece, however, the human being was emancipated in the realm of culture and the spiritual life. One has only to look at the writings of the great philosophers Aristotle, Plato, and Socrates, or the amazing expressions of individuals in the arts to see this phenomenon. At the time of the Roman Empire, the age of citizenship and the legal system, the individual gained new rights with regard to speech, private property, and voting. Thus, from one age to another, the cause of freedom was furthered, often with great struggle and bloodshed. One has only to remember the suffering of the slaves in the early years of the United States to experience the importance of freedom for the individual. The story told in history is really that of the liberation of the individual, with a good number of setbacks along the way!

Today the community has less control over individuals. In fact, its main justification is in serving the needs of individuals. What is described as yearning for community can be simply a generalization for the individual's longing for self-realization through self-development. People today still experience antisocial instincts that work against cooperation, and social structures are needed that balance the antisocial aspects of the individual. In this light, schools can be seen as a way to smooth out the corners of social life. Steiner introduced the notion of looking at social phenomena from a threefold perspective—culture or the spiritual life, rights or legal affairs, and the sphere of economics. Practically speaking, a school planning a gymnasium might take up these three aspects with the following questions:

- What will this gym mean for the community as a cultural center? How will it affect the spiritual striving and aspirations of our parents, teachers, and children?

- How will the gym affect the interactions of the people who use it? How will this interaction influence relationships with those who are not part of this particular school?

- How much will it cost? What basis can be found to maintain and support this facility in the years ahead?

If one truly respects the freedom of each person, one has to let people choose where they wish to be active, say, in fund-raising, constructing, or fulfilling the mission of a new gym. People do best what they want to do, as long as the social expectations of communication are upheld, including the articulation of a unifying vision. For the social life, what matters most in the end is not so much what we read or think, but how we act and what we do.

After countless school visits, workshops, and conversations on the topic of renewal, I have formulated ten basic suggestions for school renewal:

- The dishwashing principle. It is better to take care of a problem or an issue promptly. As with dishes in the sink, it only becomes more difficult later on. Most intractable problems with which schools wrestle turn out to have been present for a long time. For instance, in a mediation session, in which two colleagues were not on speaking terms and the issue had become so serious that the school needed outside help, I found that an incident fourteen years earlier between these two people had led to a long history of suspicion and disrespect. Only by going way back did we begin to address the present issue of colleagueship.

• Initiate dialogue, and say what you mean. Through conversation and dialogue, the school can be recreated again and again. Dialogue releases the flow of meaning so that one can work with it. As stated so eloquently by Paulo Freire, dialogue transforms humanity:

> Human existence cannot be silent, nor can it be nourished by false words, but only by true words, with which humans transform the world. To exist, humanly, is to name the world, to change it.... [Humans] are not built in silence but in word, in work, in action—reflection.... If it is in speaking their word that humans transform the world by naming it, dialogue imposes itself as the way in which [humans] achieve significance as [humans]. Dialogue is thus an existential necessity.[42]

• Rhythm replaces strength. As gleaned through this book, the old ways of doing things just do not work anymore. Unfortunately, because of our pervasive sports culture and the ingrained ways in which people respond to challenges, schools often try to force through sheer willpower something that could be lifted with a new approach. Rhythm, the graceful alternative to activity, is a way of working that enhances life forces. Rather than meet for hours on end, for example, return after a few days, work with the arts first, and then engage in conversation. This kind of working rhythm can give more to the school than most realize. Nature teaches us how rhythm is creative. Schools can use this wisdom to replace naked drive.

• Movement is healing. As I said earlier, movement often reveals the way. Begin talking, try a possibility, engage in an artistic activity on the theme of inquiry—do something and it will unlock the phenomena that will lead further. Inaction is deadening. Movement creates.

• Take an inner leap before an outer one. So often, we want to act, for action is the Western way to know the world. That is fine, but an inner act also is needed. In my school consultations, I have found that when people fail to take an inner leap first, the missed opportunity then plays itself out in all kinds of human drama. That which could be an inner battle becomes at times an outer conflict. If only human beings would do their inner homework first, much could be spared our schools.

• Bring to the surface issues for the group to look at. Sometimes a parent of teacher will ask, "What can I do? No one seems to listen to what I have to say." When this happens, it may be all one can do simply to observe the phenomena and share what you see. If something is placed on the table, usually at least one member of the group will take note. To bring forward an issue is to give others a chance to observe and begin to engage.

• Solicit different points of view, for one of them will unlock the wisdom needed. Just as there are many planets with positions in relation to the earth, so also the members of a group can offer different perspectives. This naturally comes out in a group, but it is enhanced if the facilitator encourages, even asks for different views. It takes matters out of the personal and objectifies them. In addition, there are fewer chances for confrontation, for most conflict arises when people feel that they have not been heard.

• If you are exhausted, wait for another day. In my experience, exhaustion leads to poor judgment and weak decisions. A new day also will bring new forces out of which to meet the decision.

• Following the advice of Margaret Wheatley, begin gatherings by looking around and asking who else should be there. If the right people are present, much will take care of itself.

• When a decision is made, act boldly. It is better to make a mistake, learn from it, and correct it, rather than dithering and living in the no-man's-land of the feeble and fainthearted.

Sarah rejoined her school after a long and fulfilling break. Her journey is told in the chapters of this book as she explored ways to practice personal renewal through a fundamental rebalancing of her life. It was not as if one thing in particular allowed her to heal; rather it was the combination of reconnecting inner and outer striving that allowed for the growth needed. One of the many surprises for Sarah was the immense web of relationships of her family, students, school, and marriage. They did not exist in separate boxes; the various elements of her life could be either mutually supporting or depleting. What was needed, she discovered, was a change in the dynamic, the way in which she worked with the web of life.

So often in the past, Sarah had willed her way through the day, exerting her ego and accomplishing things even when the body was about to collapse. It was as if her consciousness were stretched like a rubber band until it finally snapped. In her rebuilding, Sarah learned to work *with* the flow of life, the life forces that shape us, create us, and surround us in the natural world. There are natural times for doing things, but one has to feel intuitively the way in and grasp the right moment out of inner awareness, not intellect. Working with the natural rhythms of life became a creative path for Sarah, one that brought new fullness and joy.

In terms of her school, Sarah returned ready to exercise a new kind of leadership, one that encouraged collaboration. With the help of schoolwide training, teachers and parents began to use inquiry as well as advocacy, dialogue that opened channels of communication early in the process, flexible modes of decision-making, and mixed as well as differentiated group work. Internal and external mentors were identified, and a rigorous evaluation process was established. Once the basic systemic needs were addressed, many of the outer needs of the school seemed to resolve themselves naturally. As the teachers developed more spiritual substance, they met one another from a personal strength that allowed for better meetings. As the meetings improved, so did the decision-making. And with sound decisions, teachers and parents gained greater confidence in the school's administration. Enrollment increased, and the school finally adopted a five-year plan for salary increases and more ample benefits.

Sarah realized that renewal, both personal and organizational, requires nurturing and continued care. No system or structure can last forever, for it is in the nature of living things to grow and change. Even if the outer aspects change from time to time in the life of the school, the spiritual capacities, once they are truly awakened, can be used to meet any future situation. In the end, renewal was the most cost-effective measure Sarah's school had ever adopted.

Each school has an opportunity. Do we resign ourselves to managing and getting by with what we have, or can we strive for a self-sustaining community? This is a fundamental choice for each school. I urge our schools to summon the courage to see the *whole* and decide to do the work needed for social health. Ultimately, school renewal is about self-development, for only a community of self-aware individuals can take the steps that engender health. The highest calling of a human being on the earth at this time in history is to release the Spirit Self from the fetters of conformity to sense-bound existence. When this higher self is released, we have the chance to transcend the one-sided nature of our lesser being. We gradually can develop the ability to understand truly the phenomena around us and thus discover the objective truth of a situation. This connects us to the universal, whereas staying with the subjective personal realm fetters us to the material and separates us from others. As with all transformation, that which is released through self-development bestows the gift of humanity that is community.

The summer solstice marks the longest day of the year, the culmination of light. Those who follow the Christian festivals celebrate Saint John's Tide, the turning point of the year that speaks to human unfolding, the transition in which the lower forces, the old, are consumed and the higher potential of each human being points to greater cosmic realities. At the Saint John's bonfire each year, the students and faculty at Emerson College in England share a verse by Francis Edmunds that speaks to this new beginning:

> May the fire we light
> Consuming the dead branches of a living past
> Kindle to life in us
> The fire of love which creates anew.
> May the fire of love
> Consuming the dead wood within our souls
> Unite us with the living word of John:
> "He must increase, but I must decrease."
> So may the intermingling of the many flames
> Betoken the interweaving of our destinies,
> In sacrificial deeds of love,
> To lift a beacon of new hope for all.

Notes

1. Eric Christian Haugaard, *A Treasury of Hans Christian Andersen* (New York: Barnes & Noble, 1974), pp. 251-261.

2. C.G. Jung, *The Archetypes and the Collective Unconscious* (Princeton, N.J.: Princeton University Press, 1981), p. 284.

3. Rudolf Steiner, *The Karma of Materialism* (London: Rudolf Steiner Press, 1974), p. 44.

4. Richard Meyer, *Man and His Angel* (Sacramento, Calif.: Richard Lewis, n.d.), p. 7.

5. Ibid., pp 6-8.

6. Ibid., p. 35.

7. Ibid., pp. 18-20.

8. Bergen Evans, *Dictionary of Mythology* (New York: Dell, 1970), p. 244.

9. Nancy Post, *Working Balance* (Philadelphia: Post Enterprises, 1989), p. 2.

10. Steiner, *Reincarnation and Karma* (Hudson, N.Y.: Anthroposophic Press, 1992), p. 69.

11. Twylah Nitsch, *Wolf Clan Teachings* (Cattaraugus Reservation, N.Y.: self-published, 1993), p. 5.

12. Jakob and Wilhelm Grimm, *The Complete Grimm's Fairy Tales* (New York: Pantheon, 1972), pp. 151-152.

13. Ibid., pp. 155-158.

14. Carol S. Pearson, *The Hero Within: Six Archetypes We Live By* (San Francisco: Harper SanFrancisco, 1989), pp. 101–02.

15. Erich Neumann, *The Origins and History of Consciousness* (Princeton, N.J.: Princeton University Press, 1954), pp. 378-379.

16. Pearson, p. 105.

17. Ibid., pp. 105–107.

18. Sigismund von Gleich, *The Sources of Inspiration of Anthroposophy* (London: Temple Lodge, 1997), p. 17.

19. Rudolf Steiner, *Faithfulness Meditation*, pamphlet.

20. [Claire Blatchford], *Turning* (Hudson, N.Y.: Anthroposophic Press, 1994), p. 90.

21. Isshu Miura and Ruth Fuller Sasaki, *The Zen Koan* (New York: Harcourt Brace Jovanovich, 1965), p. 44.

22. William Shakespeare, *Macbeth*, Act Two, Scene Two.

23. Miguel Cervantes, *Don Quixote*, quoted in Bergen Evans, *A Dictionary of Quotations*, (New York: Delacorte Press. 1998).

24. Rudolf Steiner, *Knowledge of the Higher Worlds and Its Attainment* (Spring Valley, N.Y.: Anthroposophic Press, 1947), p. 22.

25. Rudolf Steiner, *Verses and Meditations* (London: Rudolf Steiner Press, 1961), p. 163.

26. Henri J.M. Nouwen, *The Return of the Prodigal Son: A Meditation on Fathers, Brothers, and Sons* (New York: Doubleday, 1992), p. 47.

27. Quoted in Barry Z. Posner and James M. Kouzes, *The Leadership Challenge* (San Francisco: Jossey-Bass, 1995), pp. 43-44.

28. Margaret Wheatley and Myron Kellner-Rogers, *A Simpler Way: Leadership and the New Science: Learning about Organization from an Orderly Universe* (San Francisco: Berrett-Koehler, 1992), p. 83.

29. Ibid., pp. 18–19.

30. Quoted in Andrew Welburn, *The Mysteries* (Edinburgh: Floris Books, 1997), p. 42.

31. From Ed Tomey, ANE Group Dynamics and Leadership Course, course materials.

32. Wheatley and Rogers, p. 49.

33. Rudolf Steiner, *Intuitive Thinking as a Spiritual Path* (Hudson, N.Y.: Anthroposophic Press, 1995), pp. 180–93.

34. M. Scott Peck, *A World Waiting to Be Born: Civility Rediscovered* (New York: Bantam, 1993), pp. 290-91.

35. Sam Kaner with Lenny Lind et al., *Facilitator's Guide to Participatory Decision-Making* (Gabriola Island, B.C., Canada: New Society Publishers, 1996), p. 34.

36. Ibid., pp 31-69.

37. Hermann Hesse, *The Journey to the East* (London: Granada/ Panther Books, 1972), p. 49.

38. Ibid., p. 55.

39. Ibid., p. 85.

40. Robert Greenleaf, *The Power of Servant-Leadership* (San Francisco: Berrett-Koehler, 1998), p. 79.

41. Steiner, *Verses and Meditations,* p. 163.

42. Paulo Freire, *Pedagogy of the Oppressed* (Harmondsworth, Middlesex, U.K.: Penguin, 1970), pp. 60-61.

Selected Bibliography

Blanchard, Kenneth, Donald Carew, and Eunice Parisi-Carew. *The One Minute Manager Builds High Performing Teams.* New York: William Morrow, 1991.

[Blatchford, Claire]. *Turning.* Hudson, N.Y.: Anthroposophic Press, 1994.

Bolman, Lee G., and Terrence E. Deal. *Reframing Organizations: Artistry, Choice, and Leadership.* San Francisco: Jossey-Bass, 1991.

Evans, Bergen. *Dictionary of Mythology.* New York: Dell, 1970.

Freire, Paulo. *Pedagogy of the Oppressed.* Harmondsworth, Middlesex, U.K.: Penguin, 1970.

Gleich, Sigismund. *The Sources of Inspiration of Anthroposophy.* London: Temple Lodge, 1997.

Greenleaf, Robert K. *The Power of Servant-Leadership.* San Francisco: Berrett-Koehler, 1998.

Grimm, Jakob Ludwig Karl, and Wilhelm Karl Grimm. *The Complete Grimm's Fairy Tales.* New York: Pantheon, 1972.

Hall, Calvin, and Vernon Nordby. A Primer of Jungian Psychology. New York: New American Library, 1973.

Hamilton, Edith. *Mythology.* New York: New American Library, 1942.

Haugaard, Erik Christian. *A Treasury of Hans Christian Andersen.* New York: Barnes & Noble, 1974.

Hesse, Hermann. *The Journey to the East.* London: Granada/Panther Books, 1972.

Jones, Michael. *Prayers and Graces.* Edinburgh: Floris Books, 1980.

Jung, Carl Gustav. *The Archetypes and the Collective Unconscious.* Princeton, N.J.: Princeton University Press, 1981.

Kaner, Sam, with Lenny Lind, Catherine Toldi, Sarah Fisk, and Duane Berger. *Facilitator's Guide to Participatory Decision-Making.* Gabriola Island, B.C., Canada: New Society Publishers, 1996.

Lievegoed, Bernard. *Man on the Threshold.* Stroud, England: Hawthorn Press, 1985.

Lenz, Friedel. *Bildsprache der Maedchen.* Stuttgart, Germany: Verlag Urachhaus, 1971.

McNamara, David. *Exploring the Dimensions of Family Wholeness: A* Handbook for the Conscious Co-Creation of Family Life. Presented at Spring Conference, April 1990.

Meyer, Richard. *Man and His Angel.* Sacramento, Calif.: Richard Lewis, n.d.

Miles, John. *Sleep.* Vancouver, B.C.: Canada: Waldorf School Association of Kelowna, 1989.

Miura, Isshu, and Ruth Fuller Sasaki. *The Zen Koan.* New York: Harcourt Brace Jovanovich, 1965.

Neumann, Erich. T*he Origins and History of Consciousness.* Princeton, N.J.: Princeton University Press, 1954.

Nitsch, Twylah. *Wolf Clan Teachings.* Cattaraugus Reservation: self-published, 1993.

Nouwen, Henri J. M. *The Return of the Prodigal Son: A Meditation on Fathers, Brothers, and Sons.* New York: Doubleday, 1992.

Pearson, Carol S. *The Hero Within: Six Archetypes We Live By.* San Francisco: HarperSanFrancisco, 1989.

Peck, M. Scott. *A World Waiting to Be Born: Civility Rediscovered.* New York: Bantam, 1993.

Posner, Barry Z., and James M. Kouzes. *The Leadership Challenge.* San Francisco: Jossey-Bass, 1995.

Post, Nancy. *Working Balance.* Philadelphia: Post Enterprises, 1989.

Rosenberg, Marshall B. *Nonviolent Communication: A Language of Compassion*. Delmar, Calif.: PuddleDancer Press, 1999.

Sandner, Donald. *Navaho Symbols of Healing: A Jungian Exploration of Ritual, Image, and Medicine*. Rochester, Vt.: Healing Arts Press, 1991.

Steiner, Rudolf. *Anthroposophy in Everyday Life*. Hudson, N.Y.: Anthroposophic Press, 1995.

———. *The Evolution of the World and of Humanity*. London: Anthroposophical Publishing Co., 1926.

———. *The Gospel of St. Luke*. London: Rudolf Steiner Press, 1964.

———. *The Karma of Materialism*. London: Rudolf Steiner Press, 1974.

———. *Karmic Relationships*. London: Rudolf Steiner Press, 1974.

———. *Knowledge of the Higher Worlds and Its Attainment*. Spring Valley, N.Y.: Anthroposophic Press, 1947.

———. *Materialism and the Task of Anthroposophy*. Hudson, N.Y.: Anthroposophic Press, 1987.

———. *An Outline of Esoteric Science*. Hudson, N.Y.: Anthroposophic Press, 1997.

———. *Prayer*. London: Rudolf Steiner Publishing Co., 1939.

———. *Reincarnation and Karma*. Hudson, N.Y.: Anthroposophic Press, 1992.

———. *Spiritual Insights*. Silver Springs, Md.: Waldorf Early Childhood Association of North America, 1999.

———. *Verses and Meditations*. London: Rudolf Steiner Press, 1961.

———. *The Work of the Angels in Man's Astral Body*. London: Rudolf Steiner Press, 1972.

Treichler, Rudolf. *Soulways*. Stroud, England: Hawthorn Press, 1989.

Van Den Brink, Margaret. *More Precious Than Light.* Stroud, England: Hawthorn Press, 1996.

von Gleich, Sigismund. *The Sources of Inspiration.* London: Temple Lodge Publishing, 1997.

Welburn, Andrew. *The Mysteries.* Edinburgh: Floris Books, 1997.

Wheatley, Margaret J. *Leadership and the New Science: Learning About Organization from an Orderly Universe.* San Francisco: Berrett-Koehler, 1992.

———— and Myron Kellner-Rogers. *A Simpler Way.* San Francisco: Berrett-Koehler, 1996.

Ywahoo, Dhyani. *Voices of Our Ancestors: Cherokee Teachings from the Wisdom Fire.* Boston: Shambhala, 1987.